Scars

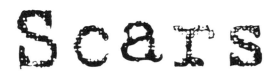

Scars

Creative Approaches for Understanding and
Coping with Self-Mutilation

Sara Martino, Ph.D.

Baltimore, Maryland
www.ApprenticeHouse.com

Library of Congress Cataloging-in-Publication Data
Martino, Sara (Sara Marie), 1976-
Scars : creative approaches for understanding and coping with self-mutilation / Sara Martino. -- 1st ed.
    p. ; cm.
Includes bibliographical references.
ISBN 978-1-934074-39-8
1. Self-mutilation. I. Title.
[DNLM: 1. Self Mutilation--therapy. 2. Psychotherapy--methods.
WM 165 M386s 2009]

RC552.S4M37 2009
616.85'82--dc22
                        2009006728

Apprentice House
Communication Department
Loyola College in Maryland
4501 N. Charles Street
Baltimore, MD 21210
410.617.5265 • 410.617.5040 (fax)
www.ApprenticeHouse.com

"Narrative Therapy allowed the group members to explain why they hurt themselves, and learn from their own expressive words. It enticed me to finally complete an entire art project, with struggle and ease. The group energy gave me the chance to speak aloud saying things I thought I would never say. In turn, whatever I said became the topic of my next assignment, with every word I learned more about myself."

— Alexandria

Table of Contents

Foreword

It takes a rare combination of clinical expertise, academic acumen, and commitment to women's development to address, so thoroughly, the phenomenon of self-mutilation. In this work, Dr. Sara Martino brings together her background in theory, research, and practice to help both clinician and client better understand and treat self-harm in new and creative ways; methods that take into account individual development and the constantly changing context of person and environment.

Dr. Martino has used narrative therapy as an intervention, and has expanded this approach to include other ways for clients to use creative means to tell their stories, reappraise their experiences, and make meanings. Given the expressive difficulties self-harmers often have, art, photography, and music seem especially germane to the therapeutic process. Dr. Martino's promising research along these lines with high-school and college students supports the use of these techniques.

As a psychology professor, Dr. Martino has the distinct advantage of teaching and interacting with adolescents and young adults on a daily basis. She is a popular instructor who knows her students, their developmental issues and challenges, and their responses to current societal pressures. Furthermore, she understands the communication mechanisms that work to maximize both academic learning and growth of self knowledge. Through her course offerings in developmental psychology, abnormal psychology, assessment, therapy, and gender, Dr. Martino is used to dealing with an array of sensitive topics in a professional and focused manner.

Dr. Martino heightens awareness, encourages scholarly debate, and challenges—always challenges—her students toward personal and societal betterment. I am certain that readers will experience her words in the same way.

— Cheryl R. Kaus, Ph.D.
   Professor of Psychology and Dean
   School of Social and Behavioral Sciences
   The Richard Stockton College of New Jersey

Introduction

Ever since I was a little girl, I wanted to help people. When I was in fifth grade, I decided that I would help other young women and become a guidance counselor. However, as I progressed in my education, I wanted more. I felt as though I could really make a difference beyond the school setting, but I was not sure how.

Since receiving my M.A. degree in 2001, I have dedicated myself to women's issues. I have worked in a Rape Crisis Center, I have worked with women in domestic violence situations, and I have done research in different areas of psychology that related to women's issues. So when the opportunity came to work during my doctoral program with women who were diagnosed with cancer, I jumped at the chance. Together with a wonderful mentor, Suni Petersen, several students including myself were able to help create a narrative intervention for cancer survivors.

After that experience, I never really stopped doing narrative interventions. I began to collect pilot data with my own version of a narrative intervention among undergraduate and graduate students using a narrative model. Their only common thread? The identity of being a student. That was the sole basis of their group to use in order to create narrative projects. But that was enough to see great progress in their ability to self-reflect and to grow as individuals.

When my esteemed colleague, Erin McLaughlin, Ph.D., called me and asked what she could do with some adolescents at her school who were engaging in cutting behaviors, I instinctively felt there was a good match with the narrative intervention. I knew that I would need to be flexible in how it was executed with a now clinical population, but I felt that working with adolescents and especially with adolescents who self-mutilate, this intervention would help to reach them. I found out later that I was right, sort of.

The group had great potential, but many road blocks. Parents were not too pleased about the idea of their daughter participating in a group with young girls who cut themselves (even if their own daughters did). Our end result was only two participants. They still did a great job with the intervention, but it became clear to me that this was not enough. They continued to struggle with their issues after the intervention was over, as was expected given the self-mutilation typically does not end until the early- to mid-twenties for many young women.

From there, the group was moved to a college setting. The idea was to expand the intervention to five to six sessions (as ended up happening with the high school group anyway) and to work with a larger group of women. The numbers are still consistently small for this group, but larger groups would probably be more difficult for every woman to have her story heard. I brought on my friend and clinical colleague, Jessica Jablonski, Psy.D., to help me run the college groups. And what I have learned from each group since I started is that regardless of the topic, these groups mean something and they matter. They matter to the lives of the women who participate in them. And most importantly, they matter to me.

What I hope that those who read this book will find is another perspective, another strategy, and another way of understanding this behavior. I care about women, and I now especially care about women who self-mutilate. Society has created the forum for this behavior. And we owe it to women everywhere to keep looking and keep working on a solution for this problem. I hope you find from reading this text that we could all be one step closer.

What is
Self-Mutilation?

Overview

The following is an example of self-injury (from the International Child and Youth Care Network):

> After having an awful day at work and an even worse time fighting traffic to come home, Joan wanted nothing more than to sit down on her couch, turn on the television, order out for pizza and relax for the rest of the evening. But when Joan walked into the kitchen, what she saw indicated that this would not be the evening of her dreams. Standing in front of the sink was her fourteen-year-old daughter, Maggie. Maggie's arms were covered with blood, long slashes on her forearms dripping fresh blood into the running water of the kitchen sink. A single edged razor blade sat on the counter along with several once-white towels, now stained crimson by Maggie's own blood. Joan dropped her briefcase and stood before her daughter in silent shock, unable to believe what she saw (Alderman, 2006, ¶1).

This dramatic account of a teen experiencing self-mutilation is just one example of a serious problem. Self-mutilation has in the past been linked with serious mental illness, including borderline personality disorder (Levy, 2005; Segal-Trivitz, Boch, et al., 2006). Other research indicates two models of self-mutilation: anxiety reduction and hostility (Ross & Heath, 2003). Still others point to past sexual abuse, substance abuse, suicidal behavior, and attachment issues (Zila & Kiselica; Waska, 1998; Krysinka, Heller, & De Leo, 2006; Brown, Houck et al., 2005). Regardless of its relationship to mental illness, it is a growing concern in our society and people need to increase their awareness of this issue and its consequences for young women.

Self-injurious behaviors, or self-mutilation, are defined as, "deliberately destroying body tissue, at times to change a way of feeling" (AACAP, 2006). It has been further defined by Armando Favazza, a lead researcher in this area, as:

> Self-mutilation (SM) refers to the deliberate direct destruction or alteration of body tissue without conscious suicidal intent. The work deliberately distinguishes it from an accidental act; self-mutilators who accidentally cut or burn themselves feel as much pain and discomfort as anyone else. It is direct as opposed to indirect methods of affecting body issues such as starvation, chronic alcohol ingestion, and or terminating dialysis. Overdoses and swallowing objects are also excluded from the category of SM. Cutting one's hand and trimming one's nails are technically forms of SM but, except when these behaviors are extreme, are of no clinical significance (Favazza, 1998, 2 of 14).

It is important to note that self-mutilation is a coping mechanism for many who exhibit the behavior. Some of the "benefits" of cutting behaviors include a means of grounding for people who dissociate (shut out certain events or memories), a way to calm down during troubling times, and allowing for a release of emotions.

Self-mutilation has been increasingly more prevalent in our culture, and especially among adolescents (AACAP, 2006). Examples of self-mutilating behaviors include cutting, burning, self-hitting, interference with wound healing, hair pulling (trichotillomania) and bone breaking (Favazza, 1998). However, there are more specific classifications of self-mutilation that have now been identified.

Types of Self-Mutilation

Favazza (1998) has classified self-mutilation into three distinct categories: stereotypic, major, and superficial/moderate.

Stereotypic: Examples of stereotypic self-mutilation include head-banging and hitting, arm hitting, throat and eye gouging, tooth extraction, and self-biting. These types of self-mutilation are most prevalent in inpatient settings, and specifically with individuals diagnosed with mental retardation (Favazza, 1998). The meaning of these repetitive behaviors is difficult to understand. It is also difficult to define what affect or feeling is associated with the behaviors. This category of self-injury is similar to stereotypic motor behavior that is seen in patients with schizophrenia. Repeatedly making the same movements, or in this case the same method of self-injury, seems to be some type of coping mechanism in clients who exhibit the behaviors.

Major Self-Mutilation: This is the rarest form of self-mutilation and usually involves massive tissue damage. Examples of major self-mutilation are amputation of genitals, eye gouging, and limb amputation (Favazza, 1998). These behaviors are sometimes identified as being part of religious beliefs and further, religious purification. They tend to be messy and appear disorganized, although Favazza indicates that an exception to that is with castration of transsexuals. This type of cutting is not related to any specific diagnosis but is common during episodes of psychosis (Favazza).

Superficial/Moderate: This type of self-mutilation is the most common form and is often associated with BPD and other psychiatric forms of self-mutilation. This is the type of self-mutilation that most people think of when they hear about self-harm behaviors. There are three subtypes of the superficial/moderate category: compulsive, episodic, and repetitive. The compulsive subtype involves nail biting and hair pulling. The most common form of compulsive subtype is trichotillomania.

Trichotillomania is a form of Impulse Control Disorder that involves compulsions to pull hair either from the head, the face (i.e. eyebrows, eyelashes) or the genitals. This is followed by extreme relief or pleasure after the pulling occurs. This disorder is commonly mistaken for obsessive-compulsive disorder, but is defined by the uncontrollable impulse to pull out hair.

Episodic is the most common subtype of cutting or burning of skin, as is commonly identified in Borderline Personality Disorder. Finally, the repetitive subtype involves using more than one method of self-mutilation in response to stress.

Who Exhibits Self-Mutilation?

Recent statistics in the United States indicate that between 1-2% of the population currently engages in self-injurious behaviors, such as cutting (AACAP, 2006). It is more common in females than males, and the majority of those who self-injure are between the ages of 11 and 25 years old (Self Harm, 2006). It has been on the rise among adolescents, although the behaviors tend to decrease throughout the 20's. We also know that there are certain factors associated with risk for cutting behaviors and they are:

1. Being a female
2. Being Caucasian
3. Having a history of sexual abuse
4. Having poor impulse control

(Brown, Houck, Hadley, and Lescano, 2005).

Self-mutilation is somewhat unique in that it is seen as a violent and risk-taking event that is mainly exhibited by females. Herpetz, Sass, and Favazza (1997) have found a link between self-mutilation and impulsive personality traits, which may explain some of the reason for this atypical gender presentation. Impulsive women are engaging in behavior that is somewhat less than typical.

Usually, men engage in more risk-taking behaviors than women (i.e. driving fast, drinking and substance abuse, and sexual promiscuity) (Wagner, 2001). It is interesting to note that women who self-mutilate are more likely to be susceptible to other risk-taking behaviors as well, such as substance abuse and sexual promiscuity. This may a result of their more impulsive nature. Self-mutilation in young women is often associated with punishment of the person (Favazza, 1998), something that has not been linked with risk-taking behaviors in men. For women, there appears to be an internal process (turning their emotional pain onto themselves) that makes it a unique risk-taking behavior. Men are typically engaging in risk-taking to externalize or avoid dealing with emotional content.

Self-mutilating behaviors typically take place during adolescence. The behaviors are seen as a coping mechanism for stress, and many adolescents are experiencing stress during puberty. Some statistics indicate that as many as 14% of adolescents engage in self-cutting behaviors (Brown, et al., 2005). Typically, a young woman who begins self-mutilation during adolescence will increase her pattern of cutting behaviors until her twenties (self-harm, 2006).

Why Women?

You may be asking yourself, why do women exhibit this risky behavior? Why is it uncommon in men? There may be a link to coping mechanisms that contribute to this problem. There are two main types of coping during periods of stress: emotion-focused coping and problem-focused coping (Nevid, Rathus, & Greene, 2005).

Emotion-Focused Coping

Although everyone uses both of these coping styles in times of stress, men may be more likely to display emotion-focused coping in initial reactions to stressors. We socialize men to avoid emotional content to be strong. Individuals who use this type of coping will try to divert their attention to other things, deny their feelings, take substances or drink alcohol in order to keep the emotions in check. "I'll deal with it later" may be a common mentality for a person who is using this style of coping. Therefore, it is called "emotion" focused. The problem with denial is that is does not address the underlying problem (such as an illness or a negative behavior such as cutting) (Folkman, Larazus, Gruen, and DeLongis, 1986). It simply serves as a diversion from confronting the problem or emotion.

Problem-Focused Coping

Women may be more likely to engage in emotion-focused coping. This type of coping style involves confronting the emotions, talking about them with others, and trying to handle the emotional reaction internally. The benefit to this style of coping is that the stressor is confronted directly; however, how the stressor is confronted may include some aggressive behaviors (Folkman, et al., 1986).

Women talk about their emotions, so they are generally more aware of them and are psychologically healthier because they are not in denial. However, the downside of this style of coping and women thinking about their emotions is rumination. Rumination involves thinking repetitively about feelings of distress and personal concerns in an effort to cope with them (Nolen-Hoeksema & Corte, 2004). Women tend to ruminate, or continually dwell on experiences over and over again, more than men. Rumination can lead to anxiety, depressed mood, and self-harm behaviors such as cutting. Therefore, it may be that women are socialized to be more susceptible to cutting behaviors than men. It is important to understand how socialization of men and women may have contributed to women being susceptible to self-mutilation. It is also important to understand what self-mutilation is NOT, by examining some of the myths.

Myths About Self-Mutilation

Suicidality: The most common myth associated with self-mutilation is that it represents a suicide attempt. Remember that the most common type of self-mutilation that teen's exhibit is superficial/moderate type. This is mostly likely to be nail biting, hair pulling, cutting or burning skin, or using more than one method at a time in response to stress. Since it involves the most "superficial" type of self-harm, it is better understand as an emotional release rather than a suicide attempt.

Some professionals also refer to self-mutilation as "parasuicidal" behavior to indicate the seriousness of the behavior. Parasuicide indicates a suicidal or suicide-type behavior that it not intended to cause death. Common examples are cutting a person's wrists or taking a non-lethal dose of pills (medterms. com). It is important to mention that people who exhibit self-mutilation are at greater risk for suicidal ideation and attempts (Soloff, Lis, Kelly, Cornelius, & Ulrich, 1994; Krysinska, Heller, & De Leo, 2006). However, the reason behind that statistic is different than some people believe.

Women who self-mutilate are typically trying to alleviate depression, anxiety, or stress. They are then also more susceptible to other methods of reducing their emotional distress, and one of those behaviors is suicidal ideation or behaviors. Some researchers (i.e. Soloff, et al.,1994) have found that women diagnosed with borderline personality disorder who also self-mutilated have more serious suicidal ideation and more recent suicide attempts than controls.

Attention-Seeking: While some may believe that young women exhibit these behaviors to get more attention, it is actually a way for the person to experience emotional release. This is typically done in private, not where other people can see the behaviors. Typically a person who self-mutilates will also wear clothing to hide any visible cuts or scars. "Self-mutilation by mentally ill persons is a private, solitary act that often temporarily alleviates pathological symptoms" (Favazza, 1987). In addition, cutting behaviors have been described in clinical populations as a way to cope with feelings of disconnect or fragmentation (Shapiro, 1991).

By understanding self-mutilation as an attention-seeking behavior, it takes away from the serious nature of the problem. It makes it seem trivial and doesn't allow for people to feel comfortable to share how they are feeling or trying to cope. However, that is not to say that there is no evidence that some cutting behaviors are about attention.

There is some evidence of a cluster or contagion effect of self-mutilation (Fenning, Carlson, & Fenning, 1995). Professionals have observed cluster effects in certain communities with suicidal behaviors and pregnancies. Cluster effect refers to an increase in incidence of a behavior (such as attempted suicide) after the observation of a peer or simply a person exhibiting the behavior reported in the mass media. Research from the Suicide and Mental Health Association International indicates that contagion or cluster suicides account for 1%-5% of teen suicides. They indicate that approximately 100 to 200 young people in our country die every year from cluster suicides (Gould, 2004).

While most reports of self-mutilation behaviors are people (mainly women) diagnosed with mental illness, there have been some instances of self-mutilation among adolescents not diagnosed with mental illness. One such example in a school setting was reported and indicated that several females were involved in cutting behaviors initiated by one young woman who was described as "hard core" and had been diagnosed with mental illness (Fenning, Carlson, & Fenning, 1995). The issue of self-mutilation is one that may need a new approach for treatment to reflect a change in the demographic of who utilizes cutting behaviors. Therapists have a responsibility to address the social forces that are contributing to self-mutilation (Zila & Kiselica, 2001).

In the preceding example, "normal" adolescents were following one individual who began self-mutilating. In my own professional experience, I have seen this phenomenon as well. While it is important to understand the possibility of cluster effect, any incidence of self-mutilation should be taken seriously and not merely dismissed as attention-seeking behavior.

Dangerousness to Others: The final myth to mention here is the level of lethality or danger to others associated with self-mutilation. By explaining the parasuicidal behavior, and the attention-seeking myth, it should now be clear that there is little reason to believe that a person who self-mutilates is harmful to others. The main target of the pain or frustration with self-mutilation is the self. It should also be clear that there is NOT a high degree of lethality for the person who self-mutilates either, as this is behavior turned inward or self-harm is a coping mechanism for difficult emotions.

Signs of Self-Mutilation

It is important to understand the myths of self-mutilation. It is equally important to be able to recognize self-mutilation in a client, a loved one, or a friend. According to the staff at the Mayo Clinic (2006), the following are signs that someone is engaging in self-mutilation:

- Scars, such as from burns or cuts
- Cuts, scratches or other wounds
- Bruises
- Broken bones
- Keeping sharp objects on hand
- Spending a great deal of time alone
- Wearing long sleeves or long pants even in hot weather
- Claiming to have frequent accidents or mishaps

Perhaps the most notable of the signs that someone is self-mutilating is the inappropriate dressing in hot weather. Scars, cuts, bruises, and frequent accidents are causes for concern and perhaps further questions, but generally someone wearing a sweatshirt and sweatpants in summer is hiding something. It warrants probing for further information.

In addition, Green, Knysz, and Tsuang (2000) found that change in appearance may be a risk factor. In a clinical case study of an individual with bipolar disorder, they found that a drastic change in body appearance was a significant risk factor for future cutting behaviors. Therefore, for women who may be struggling with self-esteem or body-esteem issues, a change in their appearance may trigger cutting behaviors.

The case study example was of an individual with bipolar disorder, and as mentioned, self-mutilation is often associated with mental illness. There is a wide-range of disorders now recognized in relationship to self-mutilation, including psychosis, mental retardation, and eating disorders. The more prevalent disorders associated with cutting behaviors will be discussed.

Disorders Associated with Self-Mutilation

Self-Mutilation and Borderline Personality Disorder

Traditional psychotherapists, also known as psychoanalysts, were the first to identify the Borderline Personality, and described it as a person on the "border" between neurosis and psychosis. This means that people with this disorder, again usually women, struggle between basic anxiety and fear to more destructive behaviors that indicate a break from reality, such as ideation and dissociation. Dissociation is a detachment of the mind from an emotional experience. For people who struggle with Borderline Personality Disorder (BPD), their experience of dissociation and ideations may look very similar to psychosis. The symptoms of BPD, according to the American Psychiatric Association (APA, 2000) are at least five of the following:

1. Efforts to prevent real or imagined abandonment
2. A pattern of unstable relationships character-ized by idealization and devaluation (also associated with splitting-which will be covered in Chapter 2)
3. Unstable sense of self

4. Recurrent suicidal behavior, threats, or thoughts or/of self-mutilating behaviors
5. Impulsivity in at least two risky behaviors (shopping, sexual promiscuity, substance abuse, reckless driving, binge eating). NOTE: self-mutilation behaviors are not counted on this criterion.
6. Emotional instability due to reactive moods
7. Chronic feelings of emptiness
8. Inappropriate anger and difficulty controlling anger
9. Stress-related ideation or dissociative symptoms

According to the Diagnostic and Statistical Manual IV-Text Revision (DSM IV-TR), self-mutilation is one symptom of a far more complex disorder. However, among many professionals, self-mutilation is always associated with BPD. Due to the emotional problems that a person with BPD experiences (anxiety, anger, impulse control), cutting allows them to experience a sense of calm or relief from their emotional experience. However, there are other psychiatric diagnoses that have been considered in connection with self-mutilation.

Anxiety Disorders and Self-Mutilation

Self-mutilation has been associated with several anxiety disorders, including posttraumatic stress disorder (PTSD), dissociative disorder, and obsessive-compulsive disorder (OCD). Both PTSD and dissociative disorder are linked to one risk factor of self-mutilation which is a sexual abuse history. Both disorders tend to occur after significant trauma such as abuse, and therefore all of the mentioned disorders up to this point, including borderline personality disorder, involve sexual abuse. Dissociative disorder involves an emotional cutoff of experiences, which may result in temporary amnesia or a depersonalization where the person experiences a disconnection between their experiences and feelings. PTSD involves more complex symptoms of nightmares, hypervigilance and a reliving of the experience or trauma that triggered the disorder. One disorder that has not been linked to childhood abuse is OCD.

Obsessive-Compulsive Disorder involves the presence of either obsessions or compulsions (or both) (DSM-IV-TR, 2000).

Obsessions are described as:

1. Intrusive and repetitive thoughts that are considered distressing
2. The thoughts (or images associated with the thoughts) are not part of the "normal" worries or anxieties
3. The person attempts to ignore or suppress the thoughts, or divert the thoughts to another thought or action
4. The person recognizes the thoughts come from their own mind (as opposed to an episode of psychosis)

Compulsions are defined as:

1. Repetitive behaviors or mental acts that a person feels compelled to perform from an obsession or according to rules that must be executed rigidly
2. The behaviors or mental acts are aimed at reducing anxiety or preventing some perceived threat

In addition, a person with OCD must recognize that these thoughts or actions are not normal and experience marked distress from them. The thoughts or actions must be time-consuming (at least one hour per day) and are not caused by any other disorder or general medical condition.

The person who exhibits self-mutilation is sometimes thought to be experiencing a compulsion to cut themselves. They feel the cutting behavior, or other self-mutilation, will calm anxiety or prevent some perceived threat. In addition, they may be experiencing obsessive thoughts that lead to the compulsion to self-mutilate.

Another anxiety-related disorder that has been identified with self-mutilation is trichotillomania. The DSM (2000) identifies five diagnostic criteria for this disorder:

1. Recurrent pulling out hair resulting in noticeable hair loss
2. A sense of tension before hair-pulling or when trying to avoid hair-pulling
3. Pleasure or sense of relief after hair-pulling
4. The disorder is not accounted for by another disorder
5. The problem of hair-pulling causes significant distress (DSM-IV-TR, 2000)

Bipolar Disorder and Self-Mutilation

Bipolar disorder is a mood disorder that is characterized by periods of mania and depression. According to the DSM-IV, a person diagnosed with bipolar disorder must meet the criteria for at least one manic episode, which entails at least three of the following symptoms that persist for more than one week:

1. inflated self-esteem or grandiosity
2. decreased need for sleep (e.g., feels rested after only 3 hours of sleep)
3. more talkative than usual or pressure to keep talking
4. flight of ideas or subjective experience that thoughts are racing
5. distractibility (i.e., attention too easily drawn to unimportant or irrelevant external stimuli)
6. increase in goal-directed activity (either socially, at work or school, or sexually) or psychomotor agitation

7. excessive involvement in pleasurable activities that have a high potential for painful consequences (e.g., engaging in unrestrained buying sprees, sexual indiscretions, or foolish business investments)

Criterion seven involves "excessive involvement in pleasurable activities that have a high potential for painful consequences". One of those impulsive and risk-taking behaviors may take the shape of self-mutilation. Also, during periods of depression, people may exhibit self-mutilation as a way to express their emotions when they are experiencing an emotional numbness or lack of emotion.

Bipolar disorder is typically associated with one or more periods of depression. A depressive episode is defined as experiencing five or more of the following symptoms over a two-week period:

1. depressed mood
2. Anhedonia or loss of pleasure in activities
3. significant weight loss or gain when not trying to lose or gain weight
4. insomnia or hypersomnia nearly every day
5. psychomotor agitation or retardation
6. fatigue or loss of energy
7. Feelings of worthlessness or guilt
8. diminished ability to concentrate or think clearly
9. Thoughts of suicide or death

The relationship between mood disturbances and self-mutilation has been established in discussions of BPD and anxiety disorders. For a certain portion of individuals who suffer from periods of mania and depression, self-mutilation serves the same purpose as it does for those with other disorders. The cutting allows for an emotional release.

Dissociative Disorders and Self-Mutilation

Cutting behaviors have been described in clinical populations as a way to cope with feelings of disconnect or fragmentation (Shapiro, 1991). It has been associated in this manner with dissociation, or feeling disconnected from your life and experiences. When a person dissociates, there is typically an interruption of the person's consciousness, such as forgetting of experiences (www.nami.org). The type of dissociative disorder that may be associated with self-mutilation is depersonalization disorder. According to the DSM (2000), there are several criteria for this disorder. These include:

- A lasting or recurring feeling of being detached from one's own body.
- Throughout the experience, the patient knows this is not really the case. Their sense of reality is intact, but there is a surreal experience of detachment.
- The feeling of detachment causes significant distress or impairs work, social or personal functioning.
- This problem is not better explained by another illness or by the influence of substances.

The purpose of mentioning dissociative disorders in particular is that the person who self-mutilates due to dissociation is focused on a different goal than a person who self-mutilates and has borderline personality or an anxiety disorder or bipolar disorder. Dissociation begins to create anxiety due to a lack of feeling. By cutting, the person is able to feel alive again and typically is able to overcome the dissociation.

Traditional Approaches to Self-Mutilation:
Dialectical Behavior Therapy

There have been many different methods established for treatment of self-mutilation. Since this book is designed to explain and discuss narrative approaches for treating this problem, there will not be discussion on every treatment associated with self-mutilation. Some methods that have been identified include: crisis intervention, humanistic therapy, CBT, Stress Reduction and biofeedback, as well as Psychopharmacology. In the next two chapters, two models for treating self-mutilation have been selected for discussion and comparison to the narrative model.

A very popular treatment approach to self-mutilation has been one developed by Marsha Linehan, an accomplished therapist with a great deal of experience treating BPD. She has developed a derivative of cognitive-behavioral therapy entitled dialectical behavior therapy. Traditional therapy typically involved psychoanalysis in which the person would uncover unconscious conflict causing distress. Similar to psychoanalytic theory, psychodynamic therapists believe that the cause for cutting behaviors is rooted in early development, and that insight into unconscious processes is a key component for treatment. Waska (1998) approached treatment of self-mutilation from the perspective that self-destructive behaviors are the result of unconscious fantasies. The goal in treatment is to uncover and deal with the unconscious material.

Cognitive-behavioral therapy is a more present-focused treatment aimed at adapting thoughts and behaviors that are appropriate in place of beliefs that were irrational or behaviors that are considered unacceptable. In 1993, Linehan published "Cognitive-Behavioral Treatment of Borderline Personality Disorder", which has become the framework of Dialectical therapy. The idea between Dialectical Behavior Therapy (DBT) is allow the client to perceive two different aspects of their reality and simultaneously make sense of them both (Bauserman, 1998). This type of therapy involves three main stages, and the client is working toward different goals in each of the stages. Stage one is centered on decreasing negative or life-threatening behaviors. The behavioral interventions at this stage would be focused on self-mutilation behaviors, as well as any suicidal ideation or attempts. Stage two involves working on experiences of posttraumatic symptoms and uses therapeutic techniques such as exposure therapy. Stage three is focused on increasing self-worth and building a better quality of life (Schinagle, 2002). This final stage is working towards recovery from the symptomatic behaviors.

Dialectical Behavior Therapy uses individual therapy, group therapy, and phone contact to work with clients on accountability for actions and also help them learn to cope with difficult and negative emotions. DBT also allows the client to process social and environmental factors that reinforce maladaptive behavior and reinforce their adaptive ones. This therapy was developed by Marsha Linehan (1993) as a way to treat borderline personality disorder, a disorder in which many people diagnosed use self-mutilation as a coping mechanism.

Other therapies have been developed to treat borderline personality disorder. One such program, entitled Systems Training for Emotional Predictability and Problem Solving (STEPPS), attempts to compliment therapies such as DBT with an approach that includes friends, family, and health care professionals that individuals with Borderline Personality interact with on a daily basis. Researchers found that while it may be a useful add-on to DBT, it is not suited to replace it or other therapies (Silk, 2008).

Important to the process of DBT to treat self-mutilation is validation (Bauserman, 1998). The therapist validates the client's behavior as a coping mechanism for difficult emotional content. While the hope is to develop better coping mechanisms for their problems, the validation of self-mutilation helps the client to move forward to considering alternatives to this view. In addition to the multifaceted approach (i.e. individual, group, and phone), the therapist focuses on four modules in DBT.

The Modules of Dialectical Behavior Therapy

The four modules of DBT include: mindfulness, interpersonal effectiveness, distress tolerance, and emotion regulation (Linehan, 1997). The course of DBT as it applies to the modules may be better understood use a case example. One particular case study, written in 2002, follows the DBT treatment of a 28-year old Caucasian woman called in the study "Eva" (Schinagle). Eva was diagnosed with Borderline Personality Disorder as well as depression, posttraumatic stress disorder, and anorexia nervosa. Her symptoms and how to treat them in each of the four modules are discussed below.

Mindfulness

The main principle behind mindfulness is observing your environment, describing your experiences in words, participation in your experiences, and developing a non-judgmental attitude.

In developing more "mindful" interpretation of experiences, it gives a person more power to cope with difficult situations. For example, one client I worked with felt great shame and guilt about her cutting behaviors. Her parents were very disappointed in her and made her feel even stronger urges to cut herself. However, by using some mindfulness techniques, she was able to observe the situation and see that she could not control her parent's emotional experience. By the same token, her parents could not make her feel any way that she did not want to. Instead, she tried to talk with parents while observing the situation as it was, and monitor her own emotional experience instead of taking responsibility for her parent's emotional experience.

In the case of Eva, her symptoms include a lack of awareness of her own emotional needs as well as her body's signals to sleep and hunger (Schinagle, 2002). One of her diagnoses, including Borderline Personality Disorder, was Anorexia Nervosa. One strategy using this model would be to focus more on her body's signals telling her that she is hungry and when she experiences satiation. This may serve to alleviate some of her restricting/bingeing/purging behaviors.

Interpersonal Effectiveness

The next module of DBT is interpersonal effectiveness. Interpersonal effectiveness involves improving your relationships with others. This typically involves coping with and changing past behavior patterns in relationships. Many people with BPD have unstable relationships that involve both idealization and devaluation of the other person. In addition, they engage in splitting behavior. "Splitting" refers to pitting people against each other. In relationships, a person with BPD will commonly get some friends against other friends or pit one family member against another family. This serves to take the focus off of the person exhibiting BPD behaviors, but also provides an outlet for both idealization and devaluation of others.

In treating BPD with dialectical behavior therapy, the person is asked to take responsibility for their own actions and set realistic goals for their relationships. The person learns what acceptable expectations of another person in relationships are and how to focus on what they want and not what the other person "should" do for them. They are also taught to improve their self-image.

For example, the case of Eva included difficult resolving conflict with her peers and identifying when she needed help from others. By teaching her skills to improve her interpersonal effectiveness, she is able to strengthen relationships with peers which may help her to seek out emotional comfort from others when needed.

Emotional Regulation

In this module, the person is taught to evaluate their emotional experience, better understand their emotion, and reduce their vulnerabilities. One of the most important things we learn to do during our childhood and adolescent development is to properly identify and label our emotions. The person who suffers from BPD typically does not achieve that, and therefore needs to learn how to label their experience and understand emotions they have not been allowed to experience. For example, because people with BPD typically express anger, they may learn to uncover the underlying emotion of shame and learn how to understand that emotion.

For Eva, there is a presentation of a commonly found symptom for women with BPD. She has what we describe as "black and white" or "all or nothing" thinking. Because of the rigid nature of her understanding of situations and other people, her emotional experience can be difficult to handle. By allowing Eva to understand her emotional reactions to situation, she can experience greater control over them. By developing alternative hypotheses to some of her "all or nothing" thinking, she may not experience as much emotional distress.

Distress Tolerance

In distress tolerance, the person learns ways to tolerate unacceptable emotions, thereby avoiding self-mutilation. The person is asked to identify ways to distract themselves from the emotion, to find activities that promote positive emotional expression, and how to self-soothe through mindfulness and meditation techniques. Self-soothing is an important replacement process for those who self-mutilate. For them, self-soothing has involved the release felt during cutting or burning episodes. By developing more acceptable means of release, they are able to find ways to cope even during periods of upset and distress.

Dialectical therapy has gained great respect in the mental health community and is typically used in some form with individuals diagnosed with BPD. However, there are many other disorders and reasons why people self-mutilate. Therefore, it is important to consider other treatments as well. Many of the techniques in cognitive behavioral therapy, and specifically dialectical techniques, can be used with any orientation. It can be seen as one powerful tool in the therapist's toolbox to combat this problem.

The case of Eva describes difficulty in identifying self-soothing behaviors outside of taking her medication and talking with professionals. The therapist working with her during this case helped her to identify more pleasurable activities to engage in during her day and found that during these time periods she has improved mood and was at less risk for self-injurious behaviors (Schinagle, 2002).

Traditional Approaches to Treating Self-Mutilation:
Addictions Model

Alcoholics Anonymous, the first twelve-step program, was developed to help people recover from alcoholism. It is a spiritual program that calls upon a higher power and fellow addicts to help the person overcome addiction. The first "treatment manual", or the Big Book, was developed in 1939 (AA, 1939). This has become a popular treatment approach for many different addictions, and many professionals believe in the consistency of attending meetings, and in the reinforcement of meeting with other people struggling with the same problem.

AA actually began as a simple process that was led by a few key personnel who wanted to help "drunks" as they were then referred. Step one was abstinence. Step Two was reliance on the Creator. Step three was obedience to God's will. Step four was growth in fellowship with their Heavenly Creator. And step five was intensive help for other alcoholics (AA history, 1999). From these simple beginnings, where much of the emphasis was placed on religion and religious education, came the twelve-step model.

The twelve-step model is more specific and allows for more acknowledgements of different religious affiliations by acknowledging a "higher power" instead of God as a specific reference. There has also been more systematic study of this model in its current form. Some researchers have begun to look at the success rate of this program. As mentioned, this is a very popular treatment method, and for some clinicians the gold standard of treatment for addictions. However, the organization itself acknowledges statistics that 75% of those who participate in this type of treatment relapse. They also indicate that no more than 5% of people maintain permanent sobriety (AA history, 1999).

Regardless of the statistics of this method, there is continued interest and acknowledgement of the twelve-step model as a method of treatment for many different types of addiction. It is even considered for use with women who self-mutilate.

The cutting behavior is understood using an addictions model. While most professionals agree that self-mutilation is somewhat different from traditional addictions to alcohol or drugs, it has been established that there is a compulsion involved with cutting behaviors. The fact that hair pulling has been classified as an impulse control disorder, along with compulsions such as compulsive gambling, indicates that it has an "addictive" quality. Although there is disagreement about the nature of the relationship, there has been a link established between cutting behaviors and substance abuse. As is shown in following two case examples, there is also the common occurrence of substituting one addiction for another one that is observed in substance abuse.

In the case of "Mary", an adolescent whom I saw in a group setting, there was the initial presentation of cutting behaviors. However, as her parents were made aware of these behaviors, she began to find other releases for her emotions. She began binge-eating and purging. Once those behaviors subsided, and treatment started for the cutting behaviors, she then moved on to sexual promiscuity. She often stated "I just need something". At times when she could control her cutting, other behaviors had a tendency to emerge.

In the case of "Alexandria", she successfully coped with cutting behaviors for a year and was doing very well. In therapy, while trying to cope with the underlying issues behind the cutting, it emerged that since the termination of the cutting, Alexandria had been using marijuana fairly consistently in order to cope with emotions. While she did not feel addicted to marijuana, it became clear that she was coping with emotions using another addictive or compulsive behavior instead of dealing with her emotions head on. She felt that marijuana was the only thing in her life that made her feel "totally mellow". She was not concerned about any of the difficult issues in her life. The goal in therapy was to learn to identify difficult emotions and cope with them without the consistent use of marijuana.

The addictions model approach to self-mutilation was developed in recent years to address some of the similarities between cutting and other addictive behaviors. Turner (2002) modified the twelve-step program from AA for use with people who self-injure. The premise of this intervention is similar to any addictions model that the behavior is addictive and needs to be stopped. By using the twelve-step program, clients can gain a sense of understanding of their behavior and lean on a higher power for guidance through the process of recovery (Turner). Many of these interventions are proven to be successful in treating self-mutilation.

The Twelve Steps: Modified for Recovery Self-Injury

1. We admitted that we are powerless over self-injury—that our lives have become unmanageable.
2. Came to believe that a Power greater than ourselves could restore us to sanity
3. Made a decision to turn our will and our lives over to the care of God—as we understood God.
4. Made a searching and fearless moral inventory of ourselves.
5. Admitted to God, ourselves, and another trusted human being the exact nature of our wrongs
6. Were entirely ready to have God remove all these defects of character
7. Humbly asked God to remove our shortcomings
8. Made a list of all the persons we had harmed, including ourselves, and became willing to make amends to all
9. Made amends to such people, including ourselves, wherever possible, except when to do so would injure those involved or others
10. Continued to take personal inventory and when we were wrong promptly admitted it
11. Sought through prayer and meditation to improve our conscious contract with God, as we understood God, praying only for knowledge of God's will for us, and the power to carry that out.
12. Having had a spiritual awakening as the result of these steps, we tried to carry this message to self-injurers and other addicts, and to practice these principles in all our affairs.

*From VJ Turner's "Secret Scars" (2002)

Although these twelve steps are very similar to the AA twelve-step model, there are some unique features for people who self-mutilate. This model specifically addresses harm to self that occurs from self-injury. The goal of the twelve-step model is to acknowledge people who have been harmed by addictive behaviors, and this may be especially critical for young women who self-mutilate. This understanding of how cutting behaviors are harming the person may be difficult to see.

This is not a program that I would recommend as the sole treatment for self-mutilating behaviors. Since the focus of this book is on creative approaches to self-mutilation, this is one treatment approach which is designed to look at self-injury in a different light. Seeing the behavior as an addiction, regardless of diagnosis, allows for a different understanding of treatment. So, by including a twelve-step model along with psychotherapy, the client may be better able to stop the cutting behaviors. It can also be beneficial to clients to feel as though they are not alone in exhibiting these types of behaviors in a group setting. It helps to reduce some of the shame shrouding the behavior.

It is also obvious from some statistics that have been done that the twelve-step program is not without its drawbacks. If the estimation from AA is correct and that about 5% of people in their program successfully remain sober for the rest of their lives, it is clear that this is not a quick cure for self-mutilation either. This is why creative and diverse therapies are needed for treating this problem. One such mechanism for creativity is described using narrative therapy.

A "New" Understanding of Self-Mutilation

The Trend of Self-Mutilation

There are some theorists and clinicians who feel that self-mutilation is in some cases not a disorder that needs to be treated with psychological theory, but rather as a means of self-expression. They liken this new "trend" with previously frowned upon activities such as tattooing and piercing. There have been many criticisms of previous "self-mutilating" behaviors that came long before we acknowledged cutting to the extent we recognize it today.

Tattoos were originally seen as decoration or mutilative behavior that was reserved for prisoners and those who were in the service. Those who had tattoos were seen as less-educated as and more menacing than people without visible tattoos (source-office). More recent studies have shown that some of these old beliefs still exist, specifically among children, but less so among adolescents.

One such study found that among children, a person with a visible tattoo was seen as less educated, more mysterious, less religious, and less attractive than the same person without a visible tattoo (Degelman & Price, 2002). These attitudes began to wan in the older sample of high school students. There was some suggestion from this study that young children held negative attitudes towards adults with visible tattoos, but that older individuals had less negative reactions to them.

Indeed, adolescents may be more open-minded and likely to engage in self-expression such as tattoos and piercings. In fact, many college students between the ages of 18-22 years old obtain tattoos or piercings (Grief, Hewitt, & Armstrong, 1999). One study by Grief, et al. indicated that 73% of their study sample obtained a tattoo and 63% were pierced during that time. In a recent study (Martino, 2008, in press), students felt that a woman they viewed with visible piercings was more mysterious, more popular, and more attractive than the same woman without piercings. There were none of the previously mentioned stereotypes that held true for a college sample with the exception of religion. Participants in the study felt that the person with piercings was less religious than without piercings. In general, study revealed that people reacted favorably to the woman with multiple visible piercings. With all of this said, about both tattoos and piercings, could self-mutilation of young women also be seen as self-expression?

Self-Mutilation as Culture

Let us not forget that many cultures have used branding, cutting, and "markings" as a sign of their culture. Two recognized forms of this mutilation are called scarification and cicatrization.

1. Scarification: the making of scars (typically on the face) which help to identify a person as a member of a tribe or culture. The process is about the endurance of pain and there are many different designs as well as many different meanings of the

scar (Awake, 1999).

2. Cicatrization: the healing of the scar or initial injury. The scar typically develops into a "keloid" scar, which form rounded elevations at the site of the scar. While typically not displayed in the United States, for many people in Africa and other countries, this self-expression is a marking of identity, of pain and healing, and of a rite of passage. It is interesting to note that this practice is actually falling out of favor, rather than becoming more popular, as the country of Nigeria becomes more westernized. "The pain and the risk of infection along with the scorn and discrimination the child may face later in life are all factors that make parents reject facial marking. Clearly, the popularity and acceptance of facial marks are fading fast. It seems that in the Nigeria of the future, the 'identity card' will be something people carry in their wallets, not on their faces" (Awake, 1999).

It would seem as though some in Nigeria have learned the "error" of their ways and choose not to scar or mark their children as commonly as they once did. Adolescents and young adults in the United States, even without mental illness, are continuing to engage in self-mutilation. In fact, approximately 4% of non-clinical subjects self-mutilate, as well as 12% of college students (Klonsky, Oltsmann, & Turkheimer, 2003; Favazza, DeRosear, & Conterio, 1989). It is possible that young women are engaging in this behavior as their own means of self-expression.

Have we as a society moved beyond tattoos, piercings, and body modifications such as gauges for ears? Is this simply the next trend? Many people have a difficult time accepting this, yet many professionals agree that most types of self-mutilation bring immediate relief to people in pain and are a means to calm down when the person is unable to regulate their emotional state another way (Zila and Kiselica, 2001).

Understanding the Motivation Behind Self-Mutilation

As you come to this point in the book, you may be asking yourself, do I know why I cut myself? Do I understand why my daughter has this problem? Do I know what diagnosis to give my client? This will also be the point in which this particular book strays from many others you may have read before. As part of using a narrative understanding and approach to treating self-mutilation, you will have to focus on the individual's experience of the problem. This means letting go of the need to label and understand the specific cause of the self-mutilation. It means accepting that the behavior exists and helping the person to create new meaning and new understanding in their life, which may in turn empower them to change the behavior.

A recent qualitative study by Sarah Shaw (2006) explored the many reasons that women engaged in self-mutilation and what specific interventions may be most beneficial in assisting them in stopping these behaviors. She found that:

> Women can and do find their way beyond self-injury. This path, however, is neither linear nor necessarily unidirectional. The journey toward stopping is an on-going process as women contend with urges to hurt themselves, changing attitudes toward the behavior and what it means in their lives, evolving competencies, and growing identities. Many of the salient factors facilitating their journeys appear driven by underlying developmental processes normative to this life phase (young adulthood) (Shaw, 2006, 173).

Shaw also found that one powerful factor in motivating women to stop is realizing the "meaning of self-injury" or simply put how they understand what they do and why they do it. How a woman understands self-mutilation and whether she sees it as a problem behavior is an important factor in treating self-mutilation. Although a very small sample of women participated in this study (only six females), their experiences do shed some light on the process of self-mutilation. And they help to lay the foundation for narrative therapy, a theory that focuses on meaning making and being in control over your experiences.

Narrative Therapy as An Approach to Treat Self-Mutilation

Recent research indicates that behavioral techniques, such as dialectical behavior therapy and contingency therapies, are more successful than medications in treating self-mutilation (McGlynn & Locke, 1997; Luiselli, Evans, & Boyce, 1986; Huband & Tantam, 2004). This book has explored two different approaches to self-mutilating behaviors in DBT and the Addictions model as modified for self-injury. While this is in no way an exhaustive list, they both represent more "traditional" models in attempting to stop the behavior. Stopping the behavior is not the sole focus of a narrative model of therapy; it is about increasing self-understanding as a different way of reducing self-harm behaviors.

One therapeutic model that has addressed similar goals is the Bristol Model (Smith, Cox, and Saradijan, 1999). This therapy does not focus on the therapists encouraging or forcing the stopping of self-harm behaviors, but rather tries to get the client to increase their self-understanding and perhaps why they cut themselves. The idea behind this model is that by the person understanding and eventually accepting who they are, it becomes more difficult to continue to engage in self-harm behaviors (Smith, Cox, and Saradijan, 1999).

Furthermore, in a recent evaluation of therapeutic techniques, the two key factors that were identified as being most helpful with self mutilating behaviors were (1) having a relationship with a key worker and (2) being encouraged to express feelings (Huband & Tantam, 2004). While Huband and Tantam did not examine broad therapeutic approaches, such as a psychodynamic or behavioral approach, it did look at specific interventions that were most helpful. They found that being able to express feelings was ranked as one of the most helpful interventions.

Given that individuals who self-mutilate can be a difficult population to work with and motivate to discuss private emotions, a creative intervention may be helpful in getting adolescents to discuss their feelings regarding self-mutilation. Indeed, some researchers assert that helping young people understand the significance of their self-mutilation behaviors may help them to manage and reduce the behavior (Swadi, 2004).

Movement Toward a Post-Modern, Constructivist Model of Therapy

The post-modern movement came about in the mid 1900's and was centered on the social construction of what is considered "truth" in society. This method of psychotherapy is one that came about around the same time and transformed the discipline of therapy for some professionals. The goal in a post-modern therapeutic context is to engage in a collaborative relationship with the client (Goldenberg and Goldenberg, 2008) as opposed to expert/client relationship. This was a great departure from traditional psychoanalysis and psychotherapy where the therapist served as the expert and the client listened to the interpretations or advice given to them.

Instead, a postmodern therapy takes place between two people working towards change for one person. According to MIND (2005), an online site for postmodern and Buddhist psychotherapies, postmodern psychotherapy is:

> Without rejecting anything, postmodern psycho-therapy is more than just psychoanalysis, more that just psychiatry, more than psychology, it is more than psychotherapy. It is "more" not because it rejects anything, it is "more" because it completely embraces and employs each of them, simultaneously, in their totality, nothing excluded, in its endeavor to grasp the Mind and to alleviate human suffering.

One specific style of therapy that is considered a constructivist and/or postmodern approach to therapy is Narrative therapy.

What Is Narrative Therapy?

Originally developed by Michael White, this model of psychotherapy involves "options for the telling and re-telling of, for the performance and re-performance of, the preferred stories of people's lives" (White, 13). Narrative therapy is part of the post-modern movement of therapy, which believes that every person has a unique and personal experience, and a therapist cannot presume to understand another person's reality (Goldenberg & Goldenberg, 2008). The relationship with the therapist is one of equal power, with the client being an "expert" on their own life experiences. Many of the struggles that clients go through in their lives are in the interpretation of their life events. Things that may seem ordinary to one person may be very significant and distressing to another.

Externalizing the Problem

The basic concept behind narrative therapy is that through story-telling, people can externalize their problems and focus on ways to cope and overcome them. Instead of believing "I am an anorexic", a narrative therapist would help the person narrate their personal story of a person who is "struggling with the problem of anorexia". This mentality can certainly assist young people who are now referred to "cutters" to explore their problem as "their cutting behavior". In this capacity, the problem takes on less meaning and the person is able to create a new life story, without the use of the behavior. "Finally, clients are encouraged to create audiences of support to witness and promote their progress in restoring their lives along preferred lines." (Family therapy, 2006, ¶ 3).

As Michael White explains, in this type of therapy there is an inherent connection to others, which helps to normalize experiences that may be socially isolated such as cutting behaviors. During this therapy there is "rich description in that it provides for the linking of the alternative stories of people's pasts and presents with the stories of the lives of others-a linking of stories between lives to shared themes that speak to purposes, values, and commitments in common" (White, 2008, ¶13).

Narrative therapy has been used with all ages and used with a variety of psychological problems. One example of narrative therapy, as mentioned above, has been with women diagnosed with eating disorders. By externalizing the problem, these women are able to create new narratives and express their emotions through different outlets. Some research does indicate that a client's subjective meanings for why they self-mutilate may be one factor in determining the termination of the behavior (Shaw, 2006).

Another leader in this area of psychotherapy is Steven Madigan and he articulates the problem of psychological stressors becoming identity. He discusses internal conversation and states that "the internalized stories we tell to ourselves about ourselves, and the stories told about us are not insignificant. Stories become us-they live us-they are us" (Madigan, 2007, ¶7). He discusses negative self-talk that many of us engage in and recommends the following questions to address this talk:

– Have you ever wondered where this terrible talk originates?

– Have you ever wondered what gives this harmful speech act so much influence?

– Have you ever noticed a negative pattern to the dialogue?

– Have you ever tried to locate the problem in a source other than yourself?

– Have you ever wondered why so many colleagues, friends, and family experience very similar negative internal conversations about certain specific problems?

– Have you ever stopped to consider how this internal talk may be the primary life-support system to problem issues like depression, panic attacks, stress, drug use, anxiety, obesity, etc? (Madigan, 2007, ¶4)

Paying particular attention to the last question, one can see how negative self-talk, or internalization of bad feelings, can lead to an internalization and identity about problems. I am depressed, I am anxious, or I am a drug addict, along with other phrases begin to become commonplace, making the behaviors more difficult to stop. One of the major goals of narrative therapy is to externalize the problem, thereby allowing the person a sense of control over their behavior. One common method of beginning the externalization process is the miracle question.

The Miracle Question

The Miracle Question is used to help the therapist and client discover exceptions to the problem, or times when the client was able to cope without the use of their problem behaviors (Parry and Doan, 1994). For example, if a client is suffering from anorexia, the Miracle Question will ask the client to identify times when they were able to cope without starvation or compensatory behaviors. For a woman who self-mutilates, this question would refer to times that they resisted the urge to cut or harm themselves. This can then become the foundation for creating a new narrative, which includes techniques that have worked in the past for the client. How did they feel during that moment? Did they define themselves in a different light (i.e. who they were with, where they were when they were NOT cutting)?

The goal in this type of therapy is to allow the client to share their experience from their own perspective. The therapist is a helper and tries to understand the whole person and see their perspectives on their life. The therapist does not make assumptions about the person, and instead tries to become part of the experience in the therapeutic relationship. This non-judgmental attitude can allow the therapist to experience the change in thoughts and behaviors of the person, as they truly understand the person. Narrative approaches have taken the form of telling (or writing) of the person's story. The client is encouraged to "externalize" their experiences, and therefore be more able to take control of them.

Appraisals and Reappraisals

Appraisal is defined as "the classification of someone or something with respect to its worth" (dictionary.com). Part of the value of something in our lives, such as self-mutilation, lies in the power of the worth or value we assign to it. If someone believes that they need to cut, then they will be more likely to continue the behavior. The goal for the client in a narrative revision is to reappraise self-mutilation and see it as one coping mechanism, a behavior that they use that does not have much worth. Instead, they can assign meaning and worth to other behaviors and activities.

For example, one client I worked with many years ago, believed that the only thing good in her life was her self-harm behaviors. It gave her a sense of peace and meaning in her world. We examined these initial appraisals through her journaling and realized that she had assigned a lot of worth to her cutting behaviors and less worth to herself. In changing her narratives, through her writing, I was able to help her reappraise her cutting behaviors as one part of her life. In turn, she was able to assign more meaning to herself and her goals of becoming a teacher.

Meaning Making

"Meaning making comes from looking at the situation in a new and unique way" (Petersen et al., 2005, 43). This is another tenet of a narrative therapy model, because a client is able to take an event that they cannot see any other way, such as cutting, and look at it differently. The most common change seen in a narrative model is looking at the behavior as just that, no longer consuming their lives, but simply one behavior they engage in from time to time. By looking at a situation in a new light and being able to make meaning of the experience, a person is able to live a purposeful life and evaluate their value system (Foa, Molnar, and Cashman, 1995).

Once the client is able to reappraise their situation and make meaning of it; it becomes a pathway to change. And this change can occur regardless of how you understand the behavior, as a symptom, as a stress release, as a new trend, or as a new cultural value. It simply looks at behavior and how much power is given to that behavior.

The Narrative Intervention Model

Petersen, Bull, Propst, Dettinger, and Detwiler (2005) presented a narrative therapy intervention targeting people diagnosed with cancer and suffering from illness-related stress disorder. The design was set up for a three-session model that would allow participants to express their feelings towards cancer, attempt to make some meaning of cancer, and integrate their emotions into their self-concept.

The idea behind the intervention was that many people who receive a diagnosis of cancer, experience internalization and negative self-talk around it. "I am a cancer patient" or "I may die from this" are common thoughts that people feel after finding out about their cancer. However, there is little conversation about this in public; many people are afraid to discuss cancer publicly for fear of upsetting the person. By allowing people in groups to discuss cancer openly and express their unique experience with cancer openly, they can make meaning of their diagnosis. They can also get back to narrating their lives as more than just cancer. Instead, they become a person with cancer; just one facet of their self-concept.

Session One

In session one, clients are encouraged to create a narrative in a medium that is comfortable to them that may include "stories about diagnosis, events associated with treatment, changes in relationships, or the impact on their lives" (Petersen, et al., 2005, 44). It is important during this first session to build rapport and trust with the clients. They need to feel that the room is a safe place for them to explore their experiences in a nonjudgmental setting. While this may be difficult to establish in such a short time, by allowing the clients to lead the session and discussion, the atmosphere in the session changes quickly into one of sharing and comfort.

Next in this session, the therapist explains the importance of creating a narrative and how changing narratives can lead to a new self-understanding (Petersen et al., 2005). The therapist will also emphasize that especially if clients have chosen a more creative medium (art, photography, or collage work) that there is no expectation of artistic ability, merely self-expression. The clients are assigned to work on their projects in between sessions one and two.

Session Two

In session two, clients share their creative projects with the group and state how the project is unique to their experience. This sharing helps to normalize their experience, as other group members can share times where they felt the same way or similarly. At this point, other group members share what aspects of the projects may have gone unnoticed by the person creating the project (Petersen et al., 2005). The therapist may join in this question and answer session as well. This part of the session allows each person to make their stories more unique.

For example, in one sample group I ran with college-aged students, a woman created her "image" using coals. She commented on her pose and other imagery created in the artwork, but it was other members of the group who pointed out her position. Her figure was set to the side of the image, as if she were not important enough to take up the whole page. As others commented she began to take a look at her project and agree. In later weeks, during revision, she created an image that was more central on the page. This is just one example of how creating a narrative of your experience not only helps others to understand you, but also can help you make revisions to your life story.

Every person in the group has the opportunity to share their creative projects in this fashion. The questions and answers help the person create a more complete picture of their self-understanding, and new meanings are made. The group is then assigned to modify their projects or create a new project (based on their desire to do so) that reflects these new meanings and understandings developed in session.

Session Three

In the final session of this proposed model with cancer survivors, participants are beginning to connect their stories with others (Petersen, et al., 2005). While it is initially essential that each person focus on themselves and what internalizations they have, at some point it is the goal of narrative therapy to personal meanings to others. This serves to again normalize the experience: the person is not alone that is coping with cancer in this case. In sharing their narrative projects, they can also focus on how their meanings are similar to one another. This also serves to expand the support group for the person who is struggling with cancer.

Finally, in this proposed model, there is room to share these narrative experiences with family members as well. It is important to note that while this type of narrative intervention was created for a group setting, it is appropriate for family and individual therapy as well. This model is the basis for the "healing without words" model, and is a stepping stone to develop alternative methods for coping with self-mutilating behaviors. While this is not intended to take the place of traditional psychotherapy, this model can be incorporated after, during, and alongside traditional therapies as another layer of treatment.

7

The "Healing
Without Words" Model

"Some women are too ashamed even to tell therapists that they repeatedly, secretly injure themselves at home and at work. Self-injury appears to be the most taboo subject to talk about, the last secret a woman is willing to disclose" (Wegscheider Hyman, 1999, 23).

This quote helps to frame this model for coping with self-mutilation. Women, who self-injure, whether or not they have another psychiatric diagnosis, are difficult to work with. There is great shame attached to these behaviors, and a secrecy that is common. Women engage in these behaviors in private, and tend to cover up their scars with clothing (source). By allowing women a forum to discuss these issues in another manner than just talk therapy, it may allow them to open up more.

Remember as it was described in chapter six, that most women who engage in therapy find being able to express their feelings as the most helpful intervention in psychotherapy (Huband & Tantam, 2004). Given the limitation of the person who self-mutilates to properly express their feelings, this type of problem requires a different mechanism to evoke change.

Narrative therapy is that proposed alternative.

And while this intervention is based on the Petersen model, it has many significant differences. The current model is split into five sessions. In part, this occurred because it is more difficult to build rapport and trust in a group of women struggling with self-mutilating behaviors than a group of "normal" women coping with a cancer diagnosis. It is more acceptable in our society to suffer from physical ailments than psychological ones and so the stigma for the self-mutilating behaviors tend to be more of a deterrent for sharing experiences. It should also be noted here that while the model is designed to be five sessions, many of the groups run up to this point have gone longer than that time. There is certainly room for flexibility in this model and therapists need to be open to meeting the needs of their clients.

The Model Outline
The Role of the Therapist

The role of the therapist using a narrative model perspective is of a collaborative partner rather than an expert. The therapist should not make assumptions about the person they are conducting therapy with, and instead should work with the client to discover their understanding of themselves and how best to them during the course of therapy. For this reason, I typically use my first name in therapy and allow the client to direct the session(s) initially (i.e. what they hope to get out of the session, what they want to discuss first or last). In using this collaborative approach throughout the group, the therapist experiences the group process and grows the experience of what others learn. The therapist becomes a part of the process.

Co-Therapists

I have always used a co-therapist when conducting the

Healing Without Words group. The initial reason for a co-therapist with the high school group was to have a familiar person in the group to help build rapport with the student participants. When I began running the groups in a college setting, I felt comfortable with the process and wanted to bring another therapist/professor into the group. This way, if for any reason the therapist cannot attend the group, there is another person who is equally familiar with the process that can run the group. Having another facilitator of the group also brings another perspective.

Both of the therapists I have worked with have been wonderful but very different in their orientations. One therapist was trained as a school psychologist and the other was trained in a clinical program. I found that having another perspective only heightened the group experience in what could be pulled out of the creative projects. Other therapists see different things in the same project that can shift the tone of the session. And if the therapist feels stuck in any group interaction, the other therapist can be there to try and move the session forward. For these reasons, I recommend the use of a co-therapist when available, but also recognize that it may not always be feasible to conduct the group that way. Once the role of the therapist and the make-up of the group have been established, the sessions can begin.

Session One

The primary goal of this first session is to build bridges between group members. However the group was formed, the therapist will work on building connections between group members and creating a safe atmosphere for holding the groups. The first session is not designed to have group members immediately share in their self-mutilating behaviors, as that can tend to be too difficult to do in this first meeting.

Rather, the focus is on:
- how the person feels currently
- why they feel they need this group
- what they hope to get from the group

Each subsequent session does begin with a "check-in" to determine how the person is feeling at present and to identify any potential crisis situations within the group. This is another important factor that is unique to this model; women may still be engaging in self-harm behaviors during the intervention and crisis situations need to be addressed.

The second goal of session one is to establish which creative mediums are of interest to each group members (see descriptions of each medium in subsequent chapters). Larger groups may have several members that are interested in the same medium, smaller groups may have a unique make-up. Clients typically have questions about how to express themselves through these creative mediums. Some commonly asked questions are:

How do I tell my story through photography (or art or music)? This question comes up often in groups. It is a very foreign idea to many people to not just "tell" people who you are. Add to this phenomenon the additional layer of self-mutilating behaviors and you sometimes get, "Am I supposed to draw my cutting behaviors?" The quick answer is not necessarily. The client is encouraged to explore their life narrative. If you could draw something, find something, take a picture that described who you are without words, what would it look like? They do not have to present finished products from the start of therapy, the projects will evolve.

What if I am not creative? This is another commonly asked question, and it was also mentioned among the cancer survivor groups. For some people, creating a narrative goes outside of their everyday experience. We are taught in our society that we tell our stories, and then other people place labels and meanings on them for us. In this model, the person is solely responsible for creating their narrative however they understand it, and it can be scary. The best thing to do is to reassure them that this task is not about artistic ability or talent. Instead, it is about creating a NEW way to understand them, one that goes beyond words.

What if I cannot think of anything? I don't know what to do. This question/comment is typically displayed as a defense mechanism. There can be resistance present in any therapeutic modality, this model is no exception. The best response to these types of inquiries is to be positive about the experience and encouraging. "I am sure you will find something you want to do" or "Take some time and I am sure you will think of something" are common responses that put the responsibility back on the client to keep working on it.

The final goal of this first session is to get group members interested in discussing their potential projects and encouraged about working on them during the week between session one and session two.

Session(s) Two (and Three)

Very similar to the original narrative model, the second session is designed to look at individual's creative project and begin the question and answer sessions. What is very different in this model is the time it takes to explore these projects. Typically, at least two sessions are necessary to allow each group member to explore their ideas fully and discuss the content. This is the point at which the therapy can be tailored to the group or individual you are working with; therapy can last longer than the five sessions discussed here.

Example Project

"Alexandria", who was previously mentioned in chapter three, was a client who began the group process with me during pilot data collection. She was a college junior and had successfully stopped her self-mutilating behaviors for one calendar year prior to joining the group. She still experienced a desire to engage in cutting behaviors and was joining the group process as a follow-up to her individual psychotherapy that was recently terminated.

The first project that "Alexandria" chose to describe her was a color drawing that she made in between sessions one and two. She had taken several art classes and so she had expressed more comfort in creative projects than some women in previous groups. In the first session, she had spent some time discussing "right" and "wrong" and how her self-mutilating behaviors fit into that dichotomy. The first dichotomous image she created was music on the "good" side and a powerful image of a razor blade surrounding by deep red color on the "bad" side. In another image, she created a rather disorganized image of what she described as the woods surrounding where she lived in the "good" side, and an image of a cut wrist with track marks from previous injuries on the "bad" side.

The discussion that ensued about her project was about what was missing from the representation: the group members pointed out that she did not have anything that had both good and bad qualities-they were able to point out the dichotomous nature of the project. In addition, the group members strongly identified with the "bad" imagery that she created. In fact, this would be the theme throughout two groups that she participated in: her imagery was consistently something that other group members appreciated and identified with time and again.

As the therapist, I too tended to identify with the powerful images created. It served to open up the group to discussing the darkest part of this phenomenon-the blood and the scars. Particularly the image of wrist that has been opened up from self-mutilating behaviors, it is a powerful image. But one aspect of the image that was missing was Alexandria. She was not represented in any way. In fact, in many of the creative projects, the person is missing from the description. See chapter 8 for further information on her art projects.

This clearly articulates the internalization of the problem of self-mutilation. Clients see their lives through the lens of cutting behaviors instead of who they really are. We spent the better part of session two discussing the two main points brought out during the session: the presence of dichotomous "good" or "bad" imagery and the lack of Alexandria as a person represented in either the "good" or the "bad" images.

It is very important considering the serious and sometimes disturbing content that is shared during these groups that adequate time is spent with each person. There is also time set aside at the end of each session to "check out". This is where you ask each group member how they are feeling and ask them to identify strategies for coping with the information shared during the group. This also allows for time to process the group content and for the co-facilitators to determine if any person needs additional assistance after the group has ended that day.

Providing "Helpful Hints" for Cutting Behaviors

This group differs from many others in that by providing therapy in a group setting, you are also allowing the individuals to share information about cutting behaviors. Similar to the phenomena that occurs with eating disorder treatment, there is a risk that women will "get ideas" from others about how to harm themselves. Recent data from the Avalon Hills inpatient treatment center outlines how women are now turning to the internet and social networking sites, such as myspace.com, to post information about bad habits to maintain the disorder (Avalon Hills, 2008).

In an effort NOT to endorse those sites that promote self-injurious behaviors, I will only discuss one site that I found to be disturbing in providing links for young women to both self-mutilation websites and suicide websites. This is the type of information that can derail the group process for these women. However, it is included here as information about what to look out for while working with this population. The site in entitled mydemons.com and it provides individuals who visit the site to other sites that encourage self-mutilation (or are in support of it), contain photography of cutting behaviors, and also some websites that are considered pro-suicide. Most women who are engaging in self-mutilation and use the internet know of these sites already. It is best if mental health professionals explore them as well to be well-informed. Therefore, it may be important to provide additional support to women during the second and third sessions. I provide email messages of encouragement in between sessions, but this can also be done as a phone call or written messages. I also provide local hotline information and follow-up with primary therapists that the clients in the group may have while participating in the group.

The best way to handle the feelings that discussing their cutting behaviors may have on them is to be open to it, and to normalize the experience. Just like any addiction, talking about cutting may increase the urge to engage in these behaviors for some women. This is part of the "work" of therapy: to confront the urges head on and work on your projects to discover new means of coping with the feelings that go along with the cutting behaviors.

Additional Resources

I don't specifically endorse any website for information on

self-mutilation, but these two have been used by clients in the past and they report that they were helpful. See the Appendix for a complete list of resources for cutting behaviors. Note that some sites are professional, but most are not sponsored by a licensed professional. View these websites based on your own personal desire.

An example of some of the information provided on more helpful websites is to follow. This information was obtained from www.selfinjury.net.

Disclaimer: I am not a doctor or any kind of health-care professional. This site is not meant to be used as a substitution for professional help or advice. It is meant for education and support.

Consider any or all sections of this site potentially triggering. Everyone has different triggers and only you know what you can read or view without getting triggered. Please make sure that you feel reasonably safe before viewing the site.

This site is neither pro nor anti self-injury. It's entirely neutral. I feel veering either way alienates half the people who might want help. I choose not to do that.

Therefore, the positive news for clients who choose to view these websites, there is adequate information about what will be provided to them and whether they are sponsored by professionals or not. Clients can choose for themselves if they want to seek out additional information online.

Session(s) Four (and Five)

By session four, each member has had time to process their work and should have started a revision to their project. The fourth session serves as a more intense look at the creative project with the revisions that have been made. The changes to the projects, whatever they may be, come ONLY from the client. They are not forced into doing anything that is suggested by the therapist or other group members. It is important to note that because it is their journey and their "revision", they need to be the creator of any changes.

By now both the therapist and group members have gained a sense of understanding of one another and are comfortable opening up to each other. By being a part of each person's creative project, the group understands each other in a deeper sense than just talking about their problems. This is the key to any post-modern approach to therapy; the group is working towards a collective, non-judgmental working relationship. Every person is the expert of their own lives and experiences. One can observe the change in the person as they start to process that they are and why they do what they do, instead of solely focusing on change because they know that cutting is wrong. They want to change because they feel they have to power to change who they are.

Example Project

In session four, the project that Alexandria created was based on her original drawings but was now on new paper and was a combination of different art techniques. In an effort to provide a more "grey" or neutral image of what she had previously described as "good" and "bad", she drew a much more detailed image of the forest. She described in detail how she loved to get lost in the woods and be with nature. Nature provided her with a sense of peace that could almost rival the feelings that her cutting behaviors from the past provided her.

In this scene, there were beautiful fall colors, foliage, and a stream running through it. On the top, however, she drew blood and the blood is almost dripping onto the page. She drew the blood in permanent marker and stated that it personified how she felt about cutting. "It will always be there" and it always has the potential to ruin the good things in her life. She drew the rest of the picture using charcoal, which can easily be smudged or washed away. The imagery was very powerful, and although the blood had not actually seeped into the scene, the whole room could feel how close it was to her.

We discussed some possible revisions to this, such as, how could we get the blood to not be in this picture? Will there ever be a point when it is not at risk of interfering with your life? Can we change the blood to not be so close to seeping into your happy places? I made the comment again that I saw no representation of herself in her drawing. It was a beautiful drawing, it was a powerful drawing but one that was missing an aspect of self. She stated, "But if I was in the picture then you couldn't see the blood." This was a powerful moment in the group and in the therapy with Alexandria. It was true that if she focused on herself more, she would have to focus on the blood, the cutting, and the negative behaviors less.

These are the types of moments you are looking for in these creative projects. You can point out things for the person that they would otherwise not notice or see. They provide you with a perspective and you can point out how this differs from your outside, observer perspective. This is also when you can start using techniques like the miracle question. For Alexandria, this could be, "How would your drawing differ if there was a scene without any cutting or stimuli associated with cutting in it? What would it look like?" By allowing them the freedom to try to create it, it allows them to take greater control over making it happen.

Final Session

As has been mentioned through this section, it is up to the professional working with the client(s) to determine how many sessions are needed to work on projects, develop some meaning around them, create a revised project, and get feedback on the revised version. By the final session, each member of the group should have completed one revision of their first project. This project may simply be a more complete version of the original, or as in the case of Alexandria, may be an entirely new project.

The final session involves a processing of the group experience and how the person now relates to the community. Remember that both Michael White and Steve Madigan stress that by realizing how our lives are similar to the larger community, we are able to develop a more extensive support system. This takes place by each member identifying how they relate or felt similarities to other members in some way. This allows them to feel a connection that again is deeper than what occurs in talk therapy. Instead of the person just saying how they feel and others agreeing, the person is able to show the group members her feelings through her project. And how they identify with them tends to be a pretty powerful experience.

The second primary goal of the final session is to encourage each group member to continue their creative projects outside of the group setting. By now, most of the group members have gained fairly significant insight into themselves. They are able to reflect on their own creations and are well on their way to revising their stories on their own. Many group participants report that they see the works-in-progress as a distractionary tool from self-mutilation. It provides them with a release and a distraction from their negative behaviors. It is again important to discuss resources available to them so that they have support in the community if they feel the urge to return to self-destructive behaviors.

Who Benefits Most From This Group?

I have run this group briefly with high school females as well as adult women in the community and in the college setting more extensively. I have found through this therapy that the projects, and the meaning made from them, are different depending on the age group you are working with at the time. While this is absolutely an appropriate intervention for adolescents, there needs to be some understanding that their self-exploration may be more limited than in an adult population. Case studies are discussed in the remaining chapters, and you will see the difference in meaning of self-exploration between the two age groups.

This group has also been specifically designed for women. To mix the group with men may change the make-up of the group and of the creative projects. While it has been acknowledged that some men do engage in self-harm behaviors, the emphasis of this group was to provide young women an outlet for their experience and a non-judgmental forum for change. Having mix gendered groups would change this experience for the worse, I believe. It may be possible to have narrative groups for just men who are self-mutilating, but it may be difficult to gain an adequate group. It has been difficult getting numbers satisfactory for a therapy group for women, and men may be even more of a challenge due to their lower numbers and the increased shame for men who self-mutilate.

Art as a
Means of Expression

Art as a Therapy

Art therapy is not a new concept within psychology. Allowing for clients to create their own images allowed for aspects of fantasy, reality, illusion, and matter to come together, conflict, and at times come to resolution (Havsteen-Franklin, 2007). Allowing a client the freedom to create without having to speak sometimes enables her to get to the heart of the psychological issue in a way that traditional talk therapy can never do. There are no defenses in art, all aspects of the work can be analyzed and interpreted. Traditional defenses, such as intellectualization or keeping things away from their emotional expression, are broken down (Diamond-Raab & Orrell-Valente, 2002). It is also more difficult to rationalize away issues that are important to them when they are created in some form in front of them.

Art therapy has been used by many different schools of psychology to handle a vast array of psychological problems. One study found that art therapy was helpful in coping with anorexia and bulimia (Diamond-Raab & Orrell-Valente,

2002), and in fact it is a therapy that is incorporated often in inpatient treatment settings. This modality has been shown to break down barriers for eating disorder patients, and has also given them a sense of control over something other than food (Diamond-Raab & Orrell-Valente). Their artwork at times brings about the inner most thoughts and feelings of the client, which can be used during talk therapy. Similar concepts have been applied to Borderline Personality Disorders, and have also been found useful in discovering the "inner self" through artwork (Havsteen-Franklin, 2007).

Art therapy techniques have been utilized for Post-traumatic stress disorder as well (Cohen, Barnes, & Rankin, 1995; Sweig, 2000; Lyshak-Stelzer, Singer, St. John, & Chemtob, 2007). In one study, participants completed a total of 16 collages and artworks as part of creating their "life narrative" (Lyshak-Stelzer, et al., 2007). They found that this specific intervention (when compared with a more typical talk therapy) was more successful in reducing trauma symptoms. Perhaps most notably, they did not find an increase in behavioral outbursts when compared to conventional treatment, even though participants had to process emotional content (Lyshak-Stelzer, et al.). This is a common misconception with talking about difficult issues, such as traumatic events or self-harm behaviors. However, talking about the issues reduces the behaviors rather than increasing them.

Humanistic psychologists have been using art and creative therapies for a long time to cope with a variety of emotional issues in adults. Natalie Rogers, daughter of the famous Carl Rogers, founder of Humanistic Psychology, developed a training program for this work entitled the "Person-Centered Expressive Therapy Institute". At this institute, clients engage in role-playing sessions, learn how to do creative expressive art, and at times also use dance and music to express, hurt, happiness, and connection to others (Sommers-Flanagan, 2007).

Still other therapists have adopted art therapy for use to uncover early childhood memories. This method is used to create new growth in the person and to allow for the person to repair any emotional problems from their early experiences (Strauch, 2007). "Art becomes a medium through which an individual can express his or her inner self nonverbally through symbols" (Strauch, 2007, 207). This increased awareness of the self is a similar concept to Dialectical Behavior Therapy, which also attempts to get clients to improve their self-concept and understanding. Therapists have been using art therapy with sensitive topics as well, similar to self-mutilation. One study conducted by Pifalo (2002) was done with children and adolescents who were previously sexually abused. The study indicated that even in sharing sensitive material such as sexual abuse, clients learned from one another and have had a positive outcome.

Some theorists further recommend that the therapist engage in "responsive art", where by the therapist creates artwork along with clients (Beers Miller, 2007). The purpose of the therapist creating art is to be mirror image for the client, to lead by example (Beers Miller). This can certainly make adolescents feel more at ease in sharing if they see that the therapist is as dedicated to the process.

The emphasis on feelings and on making meaning of feelings that are put onto a page instead of spoken is an important therapy for women who self-mutilate. Because many who cut themselves do so because of poor insight or tolerance of their emotions, art becomes an acceptable outlet for their feelings. Art therapy is a recognized vehicle for adolescents to use creativity and fantasy life in order to express themselves in therapy (Briks, 2007). It becomes a place where they can feel pain, or sorrow, without having to live with that emotion or express it verbally. They can put their pain on the page, much in the same way they put their pain into cutting. In this respect, the Healing Without Words model is very similar to art therapy. However, there are a few key differences.

Art as a Narrative Therapy

As part of the Healing Without Words model, art is a creation of the person. Many times in traditional art therapy, the client is simply asked to create a picture. In narrative therapy, they are asked to describe themselves or "tell their stories" through their artwork. The goal in art therapy is in interpretation; the goal with a narrative approach is revision. There is no final piece of art that is created and finished; there is constant revision to make sure the client understands the control they have over their life and their experiences.

There are several things to keep in mind while introducing art as a creative medium in this model:

— It is important to focus on the process and not the content of the artwork (Campbell, 2007). Let the client "let go" of their inhibitions and create their own life meanings. There is much more gained from what is said as a result of the art than by just looking at the art alone.

— Creating visual stimuli will bring up painful emotional content. This is okay given that the artwork is created within the Healing Without Words model and that the client has a primary therapist to discuss issues with as well.

— "Art" can be defined loosely; let clients choose from collages, drawing, sculpting, or any other creative art medium in which they feel comfortable.

Case Study: Alexandria

Alexandria has been used several times throughout this book to highlight the artwork that can be created. In part, this is because of the stunning nature of her talent. Another reason is because of the insight she displayed in analyzing her own drawings. She started out with very dichotomous images of "good" and "bad", moved to an image that created both the good and the bad, and then made one final revision over the course of her sessions (see illustration below).

Her final piece was one that incorporated many of the aspects of cutting that were powerful to her (mainly through color and a razor blade in the top left hand corner), the complexity of her problems (through an intricate, almost tribal-like design), and her issues to consider for the future (illustrated by marijuana and sex). This was her most intricate design yet, and it showed how she was processing what she had been through. Having made it more than one year without cutting herself was an amazing triumph. While she still had the desire to cut, she had enough resources in place to keep that from happening. However, she was also acknowledging the difficulty she was having in her life staying away from other vices, namely marijuana and sex.

She did not feel that either was a full-blown addiction at this point, but described a need that could swell up inside that was similar to her need to cut herself previously. This is the perfect illustration. It describes the progress she had made in gaining control over her life and also provides her with direction for her future revisions.

Probably the most important part of this art piece in particular is an image of herself on the page. She drew a figure that was done in all black, so there were no distinguishing features. The design almost blends into the tribal design, but is unmistakably there. She displays this image near the bottom of the page and it takes up a substantial amount of space in the drawing.

As the group was winding down from the discussion around her design, I noticed one more image. She described it as her "signature" that she displays in some variation on all of her artwork. What I saw in this representation of her signature was her. It appeared to me to be a feminine picture, it had a star and what appeared almost like a heart in the center. It brought me a profound sense of hope, as if this articulated the new Alexandria now emerging from this process. The image was small relative to the page, but it was powerful. And this is the image that stays with me now when I think of her.

Case Study: Marie

Marie was a junior in college and actually started out using photography as her creative medium (see chapter 10), but also moved to artwork as the group progressed. She participated in the same group with Alexandria. Marie had been cutting herself for many years, but had never been discovered by anyone. She attended school relatively far away from home, but transferred to a state school after she lost a good friend during her freshman year. She continued to struggle with her cutting behaviors as well as with alcohol on and off throughout college. She joined the group after being referred by her therapist. She had recently been discovered in the act of cutting by her parents. This episode was particularly bad and she was hospitalized for several days after the incident for evaluation of her mental health. She was exhibiting self-mutilating behaviors right up until the start of the group, but was working both in one-on-one therapy and in the group to stop her behaviors.

Her change of medium from photography to art displays the unique process that can occur during this therapy. The person can explore multiple aspects of themselves through multiple mediums. In her first revision project, she created a piece of artwork that included her views on cutting as a process. She is always in "process" of cutting: the preparing, the action, the aftermath. She described this in her drawing by using all –ing words up and down the page in the formation of an x. She described the x as representative of cutting.

Another interesting feature of her drawing was that she drew the symbol for the women's restroom on the bottom left corner. She described this as representing where she frequently would go to cut herself and in that way, she was representing that part of her life, however, it was much smaller than it was previously. Some of the words she used included: avoiding, waiting, seeking, findings, hiding, CUTTING, bleeding, covering, cleaning, lying, scarring, and crying.

What stood out in my mind about her revised project was that by describing cutting using all action words; it was as if she were perpetually in the motion of cutting or recovering from cutting. It was a true representation of externalization. She defined herself not as a "cutter" but as someone who is continually in process of something. You can see in the creation that she is not always cutting. She was not even always thinking about cutting. It was ONE of the action words; it represented one aspect of her. And although there was not much more on this drawing that did describe Marie, it was a start in the revision process. And the final project that she did create showed even more.

For the last group that Marie participated in, she created a collage of magazine cut-outs. This was an amazing transformation from her drawing because there was no obvious representation of her cutting. There were some things that she indicated as triggers or issues that she struggled with (dieting and body image) but it was a powerful movement from her last work. There was a lot more color represented in this image and a sense that this was the story of a woman, not just a woman who struggles with self-mutilation.

Some of the positive images that she described included the words "what if" and she talked about possibility in that statement. She also described some hiding of her true self in an ad for colored contacts. She stated, "You can always hide who you are, it's ridiculous". But in including this image, she realizes that it is covering up, and is not currently using it to hide who she is. Lastly, she discussed the possibility of the future in her creation; she has images of romantic couples, a wedding couple, and a baby.

For both Alexandria and Marie, there was great movement and information shared between them that helped them to cope with their cutting behaviors. They both shared the common struggle of trying to keep from self-mutilating and they both agreed that certain triggers made this more difficult. They also provided such rich materials in their creations; it just shows what can be done using this creative approach to coping with self-mutilation. And while they struggled with slightly different issues that started their behaviors, they found strength in each other that helped them stay away from these behaviors.

Case Study: Laura

Laura was a participant in the Healing Without Words model at a small suburban high school. She participated with one other student and was coping with behaviors that included former episodes of cutting as well as other self-destructive behaviors. Most of her friends were male students and they ran in a rough crowd. She and her friends would get together after school, in the woods or some other secluded location, and take turns "roughing" each other up. She would get kicked and punched and would enjoy the rush that came with the bruises and blood that would result.

Laura was an attractive girl but had some obvious discomfort with her self-identity. She was tall, and seemed to carry herself as though she was self-conscious of that fact. She liked darker music and would typically dress in dark clothing, if not all black. I initially suspected that she would choose music as her means of creative expression. She often discussed her love of music, but she did not use music in her sessions until later in the group.

Her initial project was very dark. She used pictures from magazines and album covers. She discussed how the music helped her to cope, but it continued to reflect the darkness. Upon further discussion, she said that she did not see much color in her life. We talked about why, and she mentioned that she did not feel much like a girl; she felt beautiful inside but felt as though others were only exposed to her less than perfect exterior.

It was difficult to get Laura to complete any revisions of her project. So during one session that she brought her project to school, I brought in some supplies for her to make revisions in the session. This is a deviation from the original model (creating projects as homework), but seemed necessary with an adolescent population that was somewhat less motivated. There were also complications of school closings that made it difficult to run the group consistently.

Once we met and she could pick some new items for her project, she stumbled upon an advertisement for diamonds. There was one large diamond in the middle of the page and she was quite drawn to it. The page was much lighter and more colorful than her original project. She said that this felt like her; it was rough on the surface, but a beautiful specimen. A "diamond in the rough" could be a way to describe how she was in her life. She felt as though she had a tough exterior, but she wanted to shine more on the outside. This was the first time that she opened up about a romantic relationship that was just starting and her desire to be seen as a woman. She discussed her beauty and ways to accept that more openly. This did lead to a greater acceptance of herself and some distancing from her friends who were unhealthy for her.

There were no further revisions to Laura's project and while she did discuss some positive changes, it did not appear to have a long-term effect. Working on meaning making with adolescents may require more time, at least for this one adolescent. It is difficult to get adolescents to open up in therapy, and having limited interaction with a therapist who the client did not know previously can be challenging. It is also possible that there are limitations to the amount of insight an adolescent will achieve. I didn't feel that meant the intervention was not helpful, but helpful in a different sense than the amount of change that college students have experienced using the model. It may also be related to the fact that many young women end their self-mutilation behaviors in their twenties. Either way, it is important to be aware of the different challenges of this model within different age groups.

The Autobiographical Approach

Journaling

Journaling or storytelling through writing is another commonly used medium in therapy. Many different theoretical approaches use journaling or some record keeping in order for clients to think about issues in between sessions and also to process information in private that need not be expressed out loud at the time. Other approaches to this model include reading stories about a phenomenon in order to allow the client to open up about their own experiences. What is unique about this medium is that there is not a visual representation of emotion, there is only the written word. A client truly gets to "tell their story" in its original form.

Mark Stone (1998) described four major principles in using journaling as a part of psychotherapy. Principle one is that each client has their own unique method of journaling, and so therapists need to open to their own style. The Healing Without Words model allows for this freedom of expression, and clients have chosen more traditional journals as well as poetry for their writing medium. Principle two is that clients need to decide for themselves that they want to journal. The motivation for journaling cannot be at the request of the therapist; otherwise the product may not be genuine. Typically, people who choose to journal in therapy have used this medium in their own lives. That has been true for this intervention as well; clients choose journaling when it is comfortable and familiar to them.

The third principle Stone (1998) articulates is the importance of the process of journaling. That is the main point of the Healing Without Words model. Clients learn from the experience of creating unique content and then working on revising their stories based on the feedback of others. It is not a measure of creative ability or the veracity with which they can write. It is simply engaging in the process of writing your life story.

The final principle is to facilitate a learning process for clients that can occur between sessions. Yet again, this is a unique "side-effect" of the Healing model; I have consistently found that clients can continue to engage in their creative projects outside of therapy. It becomes part of who they are and they can find time at home, at work, or on vacation to work on their creative projects. The process of journaling in between therapy sessions allows clients the tools "for reflection and contemplation" (Stone, 1998, 536).

Journaling has now become a process that can even occur in online communities. Several research studies (i.e. Cohn, Mehl, & Pennebaker, 2004; Wagoner & Wikekumar, 2004) have looked at the impact of online journaling. Cohn et al., (2004) studied the effects of September 11, 2001 on journaling. They found that those individuals who were more preoccupied with the events of 9/11 displayed more negative emotional content than those individuals who were further removed from it. Wagoner & Wijekumar (2004) proposed an online course format to allow participants to share their personal information about nutrition and lifestyle. The online content provides as an added support system for people who are trying to make a life change.

Journaling has also been used recently as a process for clients who are coping with trauma, similar to individuals who self-mutilate. Smith, Hanley, Langrock, and Compas (2005) reported that journaling as part of a support groups for women diagnosed with breast cancer uncovered some important emotional concepts. Clients who exhibited more negative emotion in their journaling were more susceptible to anxiety and depression post-intervention. They suggested that more research should focus on the content (i.e. guidelines for what and how to write) to encourage the best outcomes (Smith, et al., 2005).

Journaling has also been used as part of a group process. Lee, Eppler, Kendal, and Latty (2001) found that students enrolled in a Marriage and Family Therapy professional program benefited both individually and from the group process of journaling. They reported that students felt empowered by the mutual discovery of the same stressors-taking on multiple roles and balancing work and home lives (Lee et al., 2001). They felt less alone in knowing that their classmates were experiencing the same stressors. This process of normalizing stressors is also a helpful tool in therapy, and one of the defining features in the current model. Especially given that self-mutilation is such a private matter, clients feel empowered by learning that other women struggle with similar issues that led to their cutting behaviors. Overall, journaling has proven to be a helpful process whether in individual therapy or as part of a group process.

Bibliotherapy, or reading other materials as a function of therapy, can also assist the client in experiencing catharsis, but may not be readily identified by the therapist or other group members, if it is in a group setting. It is often recommended as a type of "self-help" for clients. The reading typically happens outside the session, and the client chooses what will be shared in session. One study suggested using anecdotal stories about bullying for school nurses. Once they identify someone who is being bullied, they were to refer them to reading materials on the subject in order to help them discuss their problems and identify coping mechanisms for bullying (Gregory & Vessey, 2004). For the purposes of this intervention, the emphasis is solely on writing to share in the larger group process.

Writing as Part of Narrative Therapy
Story Revisions–Parry and Doan

Parry and Doan (1994) suggested a narrative model that encourages therapists to help clients "author" their own stories. While some of the techniques are ones that have already been described as narrative techniques (i.e. the miracle question, externalizing the problem), some are unique to their model. The first concept of interest that could be applied to a Bibliotherapy technique is uniting personal stories with the stories of others (Parry & Doan, 1994).

In this task, one of the central features of uniting your story is to understand your personal story well enough to determine how they play a role in other people's stories. For example, an individual has to know their story well enough to know how being their mother and father's daughter plays a role in their stories. This allows them to think beyond their immediate existence and look to how their lives also impact others. While this could technically be done with any creative medium, by having your story written or even reading your story to others, it helps to solidify the concepts for the client. There is a document on record that represents a draft. This draft can be edited and changed to include other roles and other people that contribute to the story.

Another task in Parry and Doan's model is to examine "conflicting stories" rather than discussing people in conflict. This can be especially helpful for adolescents who often feel "at odds" with parents and loved ones. By understanding how communication patterns or conversation are in conflict, it allows the person more control over changing the situation. If the person believes they are in "in conflict" with their parents, they may be unwilling or unable to see how they could change. However, if one story about missing curfew is in conflict, then the relationship can be changed more easily.

Case Study: Mary

Mary was one of the participants from the college groups and was a college sophomore. She had not exhibited any active cutting behaviors for over a year, but joined the group to make some meaning of why she cut herself and also to hopefully help other young women who were actively cutting themselves.

She chose writing as her medium, and focused mainly on poetry as her means of expression. Her first piece of work was to develop a poem that was written using the letters in her name. This way, she developed a type of mantra that she could remember and reference easily. The other members of the group did identify with this method as it became something that could be easily remembered and used to calm the person to prevent future cutting behaviors-almost serving as a delay mechanism.

In an effort to maintain her confidentiality, her name was removed from her poem, but the rest of the content "life at nineteen" is documented below:

Live *my life.*
I *look into my*
Future *and do not look back.*
Everything *I had gone through,*

A *past not*
To *be repeated, but go forward with my life.*

Not *to do, but carry with me what*
I *had done.*
Nothing *can stop me now.*
Everything *I do from*
This *day forth will be the better me and*
Enjoy *the life I am meant to live.*
Empowering *me to live my life and*
Not *go back to the life I once lived.*

As the group progressed, she moved into more traditional journaling. The other members of the group and facilitators could feel the stress in how the journal entries were written. The student clearly articulated stressors from schoolwork, home life concerns, and trying to strike a balance between her family and herself as a young woman. Very similar to Lee et al. (2001), the other group members really identified with this particular form of journaling. They could see themselves in each of her entries, perhaps a slightly different story line, but the common themes of multiple roles and stressors were the same.

The main difficulty that I encountered with Mary while working with her journaling was that there really wasn't any rewriting of her story. She would continue to journal, and the content would be modified somewhat, but it was not the same experience of change that happened with clients who chose other mediums. With a drawing or photography, or even a music CD, you can readily see the revision of the story. The process of journaling may be slower and less obvious to group members, and so perhaps it was more challenging to incorporate in a short intervention.

One great outcome of having Mary in one of my groups was that she benefited and gain different things from other members. She was able to provide other group members with hope and a look toward her future. She was resolved not to engage in self-mutilating behaviors any more, and was working on activism to prevent this problem from occurring in other women. At the same time, she learned what she had accomplished from the other members of the group. They would comment on how difficult it was for them to stop self-mutilating and she would be reminded of her accomplishments. She was also reminded at times that she had more work to do in her life, which would jumpstart further writing for her.

This is part of the benefit of a narrative approach to treatment. the group is ever-evolving and so this type of change in one person's behavior is beneficial. The group does not have to have the same reality to start (all actively cutting) to mutually benefit and discover things about themselves together.

Case Study: Olivia

Olivia was a high school participant who also focused on poetry as her means of expression. She had a history of cutting behaviors, as well as binging and purging and sexually promiscuous behaviors. She was a sophomore in high school at the start of the group process, and was heavily focused on relationships with men during the intervention. Part of her difficulty was that she did not have a strong self-image. Therefore, along with cutting behaviors, she did not feel as though she was worthy of a good partner. She continually engaged activities with males who treated her as a means to have needs met.

She was engaging in promiscuous sexual behavior and at times struggled with eating disturbances. She would binge and purge in times of stress. She was talkative during the groups about issues going on at school, but was very difficult to engage in therapy. She was a textbook adolescent case in that sense; she was unwilling to trust and explore her issues further.

Olivia represented a unique challenge, because she was difficult to engage in the creative aspect of the project. We would meet, discuss possible ideas for project, and then meet the next week. She never presented with any project. This occurred a few times and the group was extended to accommodate this. Due to her initial resistance, I set up a group where the supplies for creating a project readily available.

It was during this session that she presented a poem that she had written. She explained that she was concerned about sharing because she felt as though she would get in trouble for the content of the poem. The poem contained pretty graphic sexual content; the main theme of the poem was sexual activity being compared to and with a shiny gun. While there was no mention of any suicidal intent, I still had to explore this theme further. She insisted that she was not suicidal, but rather felt that a gun was highly sexual and so she used it as a medium to describe her strong feelings of sexuality.

We spent the latter part of that session trying to explore how she could describe herself more deeply outside of her sexuality. She was so focused on sex and sexuality that part of her was missing from the process. Who was she? How did she feel about herself? She didn't know. This was tough for her to work through and the intervention did not allow her to get to the point that she knew herself well. However, it did allow her to see that by focusing all of her time and energy on males and on sexuality, she was not finding out who she was. More importantly, she was not engaging in trying to determine who she would be in the future.

Photography as a Means of Expression

Photography as an Art

Photography has long been a form of art in society. From displays of professional photography to the trend of printing digital pictures in a home, photography is a means of self (and other) expression. What has been missing from the psychological literature is how photography could be used in therapy. Art therapy has been examined thoroughly in previous chapters, but there is often relatively little information on the medium of photography in psychotherapy.

Photography as a Therapy

One study by Hanieh and Walker (2007) reported that photography was a successful means of describing "who are you" in both depressed patients and a control group. While the depressed clients had a more constricted view of themselves, both groups enjoyed using photography as their medium. They felt that by using photography (a novel concept) rather than other nonverbal means (such as questionnaires), it would allow clients to express themselves more fully.

Judy Weiser (2001; 2007; 2008) created a phototherapy, in which clients learn about themselves through their photographs. Using a constructivist perspective again, the photos can unlock meaning for the client and help him or her to see their lives differently. She describes five techniques to her model of phototherapy. The techniques involve different types of photography, such as:

1. Photos that were taken by the client. This can be used to create a third person viewpoint of the individual's life experiences. They do not have to be the subjects of the photos, but rather their life becomes the subject of the photo.

2. Photos that were taken of the client by other people. This provides a perspective from the person taking the picture, and the photographer typically has had creative freedom over the picture.

3. Self portraits. These pictures are taken of the client by the client. They can also be metaphorical representations of "self".

4. Family album collections. The idea behind these collections of photographs (they do not have to be in albums necessarily) is to present a family narrative or a perosnal history of the client through photographs.

5. "Photo-projectives". These photos can be any images that the client has identified with or put some specific meaning onto in the course of therapy. This projective technique is all about how the client interprets the image (Weiser, 2001).

Photography inherently is a constructive approach to therapy in that the photographs, even self-portraits, are merely representations of reality. Together, the client and therapist must interpret what is in the photograph and together they can develop a shared meaning of the pictures. This is especially important to women who self-mutilate, which is such a private behavior. Clients do not necessarily have to take pictures of their self-destructive behaviors, but rather can express how they feel or who they are that make them feel as though they have to cope with cutting behaviors. The client can reach a unique level of self-disclosure without having to physically show their scars or talk about how they feel during the episodes. This type of freedom in communication can strengthen the bond and trust between client and therapist. This has been found for women who self-mutilate-the most important aspect of psychotherapy is being able to trust their therapist and share their experiences (Huband & Tantum, 2004).

Case Studies: Pilot Data

Before I even started running groups for self-mutilation, I would have groups of undergraduate and graduate students complete the narrative intervention to collect some pilot data to measure its effectiveness. I found that groups of students could come up with a very simplistic "shared" identity, such as being a student, and develop very elaborate projects based on the concept.

One student in particular, Paula, developed a narrative project using photography to express her life as a mother and a graduate student. She developed 12 photographs that represented her life and the difficulties she experienced day to day. She felt as though she was overwhelmed with her multiple roles. The best part of her project, and the reason for mentioning it, is that she had photographs that were of her in the third person. This represents technique one according to Weiser's model (2001), where all of the work involves photos taken by the client.

Although the actual pictures cannot be included her for confidentiality concerns, I have included some photographs of my own as examples. She created images such as her office/ playroom/living room and the representation of the stress of motherhood, school, and work was there. You could see how the multiple uses for one room in her house were very similar to the "multiple" roles in her life.

This one student's example has always stood out in my mind because it was a great representation of the narrative project, but also because it felt so real. It was as if you had the camera and could see into the other person's mind. Photography can indeed be a very personal medium in which to explore their lives and psychological issues.

Case Study: Maria

Maria, one of my college participants mentioned in chapter eight, chose among her various art forms (collage, drawing) to create a collage of photographs. This could be likened to Weiser's (2001) "family album" concept. The photo collage was actually the first project that she chose to do. In the collage, she used photographs of friends, family, famous individuals (magazine cut-outs), and in the center, she had a picture of a smiley face. This face she told us was to represent the façade that she put on for everyone in her life. In all of the other photographs of the collage, she was not smiling. But this bright yellow smiley face was there, right in the center, and was the largest image on the page.

Again, this project could not be copied and presented because of confidentiality, but the image was very powerful. What the project lacked, in its first form, was an understanding of who she really was. The yellow smiley face stood out as such a "fake" representation that it was difficult to determine where the real Maria was beyond that. This was very difficult for Maria to overcome; she couldn't create an image for herself that she liked and felt was genuine using photography. It was at this point that she changed projects.

This is not uncommon in therapy; you touch upon an issue that is very close to the heart (poor self- image or self-understanding) and the client develops some resistance. It was difficult for Maria to explore who she was under the façade. It was an issue that she continued to struggle with in group; in part because she was always the daughter, friend, sister that everyone liked and felt was a "good girl" while inside she was struggling. She had successfully cut herself in secret for years.

In her first project, we did not uncover her true self or "cure" her of the urge to cut. But what we did do, especially through the very personal medium of photography, was to get to the heart of the issue very quickly for her. In her later projects, she continued to process more deeply the idea of who she was in contrast to whom she felt others wanted her to be.

Issues of Confidentiality

The potential problem with photography, especially when the photography shows "first person" experiences, is confidentiality. There is the possibility of having groups where young women know each other or know some people in common. Therefore, there are sometimes images that reveal something personal about others. In this case, the therapist should reaffirm among the participants that confidentiality is important and that clients should not share any of the information viewed during the intervention with other people.

The other difficulty is in sharing this medium with other therapists. There are many powerful examples that would have been interesting to include in this book, but are impossible because they need to be kept confidential. That is the double-edged nature of photography in therapy; it is a very powerful medium to use and effect change, but is sometimes too personal to share with others.

Music as a Means of Self Expression

Music and Memory

Music can affect our memories. Almost everyone can turn on the radio, hear a song from a particular point in time, and attach a personal memory to that song or that time period. The phenomenon is called context-dependent memory and it essentially means that we remember certain things in their original context. For example, if you are listening to a certain song, a certain tempo, or perhaps a certain key of music, during an important event, you remember it in that context. If you were to change the context in which the event was remembered, it may result in forgetting the material. However, typically having similar content (i.e. the same song) will improve recall of past events.

Balch and colleagues in several studies (i.e. 1992; Balch and Lewis, 1996) have explored the effect of key change, the tempo of music, the timbre of music, and mood of the music in relationship to context-dependent memory and found that there are many different factors about music that can impact recall of events. The important aspect to remember for the therapeutic relationship is that clients may need exposure to the same music in order to avoid context –dependent memory concerns.

Basically, the same rules apply to this creative medium as they did for journaling. The therapist cannot simply play an array of music in hopes of generating a connection to their clients' lives or even to their self-mutilating behaviors. This has to be a creative medium that clients are familiar and comfortable with; i.e. they typically use music to calm them when they are in crisis or that they use music to improve their memory of events.

Music as a Therapy to Enhance Meaning Making

According to the American Music Therapy Association (AMTA), music therapy is:

> Music Therapy is an established health profession in which music is used within a therapeutic relationship to address physical, emotional, cognitive, and social needs of individuals. After assessing the strengths and needs of each client, the qualified music therapist provides the indicated treatment including creating, singing, moving to, and/or listening to music. Through musical involvement in the therapeutic context, clients' abilities are strengthened and transferred to other areas of their lives. Music therapy also provides avenues for communication that can be helpful to those who find it difficult to express themselves in words. Research in music therapy supports its effectiveness in many areas such as: overall physical rehabilitation and facilitating movement, increasing people's motivation to become engaged in their treatment, providing emotional support for clients and their families, and providing an outlet for expression of feelings. (www.musictherapy.org/quotes.html, ¶2).

Just like the many other examples provided, music as an avenue for therapy provides a means for client to express themselves in a non-threatening manner. The nonverbal communication of music can be just as powerful as the spoken word. When used in the correct context, music can be a powerful edition to the Healing Without Words model. Many people in a group setting can relate to music; especially when clients use current music. By playing music, instead of using words, there is a feeling of instant ice breaker. Clients begin to share what they feel or remember when hearing the music. This can bring new meaning to the client who chose the songs.

Take for example a song of empowerment, such as "I will survive." The client may have selected this particular song because of its meaning of strength in a romantic relationship. However, another client, just hearing the song again after a long period of time, may find meaning related to coping with difficult parents, another in dealing with school stressors, and still others relating to overcoming self-mutilation. In this one song, a client was able to describe who he or she is, get some alternative meanings for their experience, and be able to begin revisions to their story based on feedback from other clients.

Case Studies: Pilot Data with College Students

I have not had many clients choose this medium as their means of expression up to this point. I have, however, experienced some pretty powerful CDs that were made by students as part of my pilot data. One student in particular developed songs that described what her life was like as a student. Some of the songs that she chose included: "Stuck in the Middle with You", "I Still Haven't Found What I'm Looking For", "Unwell", and "A Bad Day". In addition to playing the music in the group session, she also provided the lyrics to each student. There was a low murmur among the group as students began relating to each other what different songs meant to them, how they now related them to being a student, and how they enjoyed certain songs. They were quieter when they did not know the song, somber when the lyrics were deeper or sad, and quite verbose when the song was happy or one that most of them could connect to their own lives.

It became one of the liveliest sessions of the group, and I was encouraged that many future participants would choose this medium. The reasons I think that this may not have happened could be the private nature of some song lyrics; i.e. some clients may feel that they need to find songs that discuss self-mutilation or self-harm in some form. It may also be that burning a CD just takes more time and money to create than perhaps artwork or journaling.

Case Study: Laura

Laura has been previously described in using art as a creative medium. As a high school student, and one who is definitely interested in music, I had thought that she may choose music as her creative medium. Indeed, during the first group session she described different options in creating music. But she never actually shared any music in beginning sessions. However, towards the end of her group sessions, she shared with me on her IPOD some songs that she felt described her well.

The genre of music that she was most interested in was a very hard heavy metal. She played some songs from the group Korn and stated how they sang was almost as important as what they sang. She felt that they sang with force and strength and this is the way she wanted to be in her own life.

I found this moment very powerful, because up to this point I had focused on what songs were chosen and how the lyrics represent the person's story. This song, however, was most representative of her life and what she wanted to be because of how it was sung. It was another moment when I realized that whatever creative project that clients will choose, there is something new to learn; a new perspective to be seen. That is what is most important about a narrative, constructivist perspective. The client(s) and therapist are learning their own realities together and are making meaning together.

Coping in the Long-Run

The Healing Without Words model is a short-term intervention that is designed to help women who struggle with self-mutilation change. It is not designed to be a cure to a very serious problem. It is not designed to explain what self-mutilation is, or to necessarily delve into the deeper issues, such as trauma and abuse, that may have led to self-mutilation. Therefore, it is important for each person who is struggling with this problem, and professionals who may work with them, to keep several principles in mind when dealing with self-mutilation in the long-run. The first of these is to explore self-mutilation further.

Understanding Self-Mutilation

An important first step to coping with self-mutilation is beginning to understand the motivation behind the problem. As has been described throughout this book, some women self-mutilate as one symptom that is part of a larger disorder. In order to discover if there is an underlying mood, anxiety, or personality disorder, a person needs to go through a thorough assessment with a mental health professional. By targeting what disorder may be triggering the behavior, the client is one step closer to understanding themselves and coping with the problem. However, not every person who self-mutilates engages in this behavior has a mental illness. The reasons behind the self-mutilation in these cases may be even more important to understand.

Cutting as a cultural phenomenon is another interesting perspective into this behavior that has been discussed in the book as well. There have been similar attitudes, such as negative reactions or associations to mental illness, that in the past were related to tattoos and visible piercings. It could be that self-mutilation will be more acceptable in future generations. The person needs to be clear in this case that self-mutilation is about self-expression in this case. I don't believe that we have enough information at this point to determine, as a profession, if cutting can strictly be a form of self-expression.

Perhaps the most alarming reason for self-mutilation that has been identified is cutting behaviors that are the result of a cluster effect. While there are few sources that describe this happening (i.e. source here), clinically it appears that is happening often. There have been several high schools that I have visited in recent years that have described a cluster effect for self-mutilation. "There are a group of them that cut themselves" and "she is one of those who just does it for attention" are common phrases that I hear in relationship to this problem. However, this is a serious behavior, regardless of the motivation.

Whether you are a client who thinks you may self-mutilate because of your friends or a therapist working with someone you expect may be a product of a cluster effect, this is an important problem to explore. There is some underlying issue that caused this particular behavior to be exhibited. Therefore, it is still very important to explore the issue further.

Continuing Therapy

Using a narrative technique, such as Healing Without Words, is a great adjunct for therapy. A client can take the skills that they learn during the group process to continue in their long-term therapy. For some people who may be reading this book and have not yet sought out therapy, it is important to pursue therapy in addition to this intervention.

How do you seek out therapy? The first goal will be to find a therapist whose orientation will work best for your problems. Two models that have been used to cope with self-mutilation (and were described in this book) are Dialectical Behavior Therapy and using an Addictions model. However, there are many more approaches to this problem.

Some previously used therapies for self-mutilation include crisis intervention, especially for clients who have just engaged cutting behaviors. Crisis intervention involves short-term counseling that typically occurs pretty soon after the cutting behavior (the crisis in this model) has happened. The goal of this approach is provide supportive counseling, give some education to the client about their crisis, and to help them problem-solve in the short term. Crisis intervention is an intensive and supportive intervention for the short run, but there may need to be additional therapies to continue coping with self-mutilation.

Other methods of therapy that have been used in dealing with self-mutilation are:

- Stress Reduction
- Family Therapy
- Medication (in conjunction with therapy)
- Add more from powerpoint

Focusing on Externalization

In coping with self-mutilation in the long-run, it may become a helpful reminder to clients that if they focus on externalizing the behavior, they can gain more control over it. This type of problem has become one that the media has turned into an identity. "I am a cutter" or " the new crisis of cutters" makes the behavior seem as though it is a part of the person. This makes it very difficult to treat. By simply remembering to separate "I am a cutter" from "I sometimes cut when I am stressed" or "Cutting is one coping mechanism I have used", a client changes the perspective. There is much more control that can exerted over a behavior than a personal attribute. It is a helpful tool to keep in mind.

Helping Women Cope with a Women's Issue

In an ideal world, what would help women cope with self-mutilation in the long-run would be to change some of the pressure that we have put on women in recent years. From the superwoman complex to the emergence of eating disorders, there has been a significant backlash against women. Most of this backlash is suffered as a reaction to feminism. As women have accomplished more, we continue to make them suffer by creating unattainable ideals of weight and motherhood.

At the same time, women have been encouraging their girls to achieve more and more. The reaction? Many women are opting to stay at home or "opt out" of the workforce in an effort to lead a simpler life, as they did in the past. this carries with it serious consequences as authors such as Ainsworth (2007) point out. Women who depend on their partners to survive are experiencing problems supporting themselves after divorce or death, and are frustrated when they want to enter back into an unwelcoming workforce.

Another note to keep in mind that specifically applies to

women who self-mutilate is relationships. Many times, self-mutilation is related to past trauma and abuse, so moving forward with intimate relationships can be difficult. According to others who have written books on this topic (i.e. Levenkron, 1998; Wegscheider Hyman, 1999; Smith, Cox, and Saradijan, 1999), many times loved ones do not know how to cope with the cutting behaviors and they react out of fear. It is difficult for women who experience self-mutilation to trust others and establish intimacy (Wegscheider Hyman, 1999) and so it is important in coping with this problem in the future to understand how others may react to the problem.

Some tips for helpful responses that loved ones of a woman who self-mutilates can give her are:

1. Do not be judgmental: it is normal to be disturbed, concerned, upset, disappointed, or afraid that someone is cutting themselves. It is not a helpful response to tell them that as your initial reaction. Try to find out as much information as you can, and take it in. You can express your concern for what they may be going through and be supportive of their efforts to stop.

2. Love them: it is important for someone who self-mutilates to feel as though they are loved and supported unconditionally. Many of them have dealt with individuals who broke their trust and hurt them, so your unconditional regard will provide a positive relationship in their lives.

3. Try to overcome your fear: it is clear from the media and from people in general that the topic of self-mutilation is taboo and is considered a suicidal behavior. Try to overcome your own fears about what the self-mutilation may mean or what you may witness by knowing someone who self-mutilates.

They need your support more than taking on your fears as well as their own.

Until there are more statistics that reflect the trend is changing, self-mutilation continues to be a women's issue. the reasons for turning harmful behavior inward, as many who self-mutilate do, are not entirely clear at this point. It is clear that the method of self-harm appears to be gendered. Women do not behave aggressively as much as men, but they are harming themselves in ways that can be far worse. Therefore, it is important to even more information about this behavior to help prevent it for future generations of women.

Moving Forward

The final thing that will help clients to cope with this problem is to open up about their experiences. Researchers know that this problem is not forever, in fact, most females stop this behavior by the time they reach 25 years old. It helps to keep it in perspective; knowing that this too shall pass. Any person, client or therapist, can begin to process the experience of self-mutilation in this context and again gain a sense of control.

While it may not make it completely better in the long-run to know that self-mutilation does not last forever, it is another reminder to keep while you are doing all of the other things. Whether you are at the end of the therapeutic journey or just beginning, there is hope. This experience is just one day in the reality of life that is created, and changed, every day.

Appendix
Additional Resources

Books
There are both scholarly books on self-mutilation as well as memoirs that have been reviewed and seen as helpful for people who self-injure.

Alderman, T. (1997). *The Scarred Soul: Understanding & Ending Self-Inflicted Violence.* Oakland, CA: New Harbinger Publications.

Bowman, S., & Randall, K. (2004). *See My Pain: Creative Strategies and Activities for Helping Young People Who Self-Injure.* Chapin, SC: Youthlight, Inc.

*Carney, M. (2005). *Stitched: A Memoir.* New York: Publish America.

Favazza, A. (1996). *Bodies Under Siege: Self-Mutilation and Body Modification in Culture and Psychiatry.* Baltimore, MD: The Johns Hopkins University Press.

Levenkron, S. (1998). *Cutting: Understanding and Overcoming Self-Mutilation.* New York: Norton and Co., Inc.

*Robson, A. (2007). *Secret Scars: One Woman's Story of Overcoming Self-Harm.* New York: Authentic.

Shapiro, L. (2008). *Stopping the Pain: A Workbook for Teens Who Cut and Self-Injure.* Oakland, CA: New Harbinger Publications.

Turner, V.J. (2002). *Secret Scars: Uncovering and Understanding the Addiction.* Center City, MN: Hazelden.

*Vega, V. (2007). *Comes the Darkness, Comes the Light: A Memoir of Cutting, Healing, and Hope.* New York: AMACON.

Walsh, B. (2005). *Treating Self-Injury: A Practical Guide.* New York: Guilford Publications.

Note: autobiography that may contain sensitive material

Web Sites

This is not an exhaustive list of sources that can be found online. Most of the sites are NON-professional, but have been put together by those who suffer from self-injury or those who want to help those who self-injure.

www.palace.net/~llama/psych/injury.html
- Self-injury: You are NOT the only one
- This website provides information on cutting

behaviors, provide links to other books
and information, as well as an interactive
questionnaire to determine whether you
engaging in self-mutilation.

www.self-injury.net
- Site developed by a woman who self-injures that
  provides insight and information from other
  women who struggle with this issue.

www.focusas.com/Selfinjury.html#Help_and_Support
- Focus Adolescent Services
- Information, definitions, and resources for
  coping with self-mutilation

www.nshn.co.uk
- National Self-Harm Network (UK)
- NSHN is a registered charity that was started
  ten years ago to raise awareness on this issue.
  Those who created the site either engaged in
  self-harm or saw in their families or friends.

www.selfmutilatorsanonymous.org
- 12-step program for self-mutilation
- This site provides 12-step program information
  for self-mutilation that includes online meetings
  if you cannot find a meeting in your area.

www.twloha.com/index.php
- To Write Love on Her Arms
- A moment to raise awareness about cutting
  behaviors that started based on one woman's
  struggle that has now become a larger
  movement.

References

Alderman, Tracy (2006). Self-Inflicted Violence: Helping those who hurt themselves. *The International Child and Youth Care Network*. Last accessed 5/30/08 at: http://www.cyc-net.org/reference/refs-self-mutilation-alderman1.html.

American Academy of Child and Adolescent Psychiatry (AACAP) (2006). Self-Injury in Adolescents. Retrieved on 5/30/08 at: http://www.aacap.org/publications/factsfam/73.htm .

American Music Therapy Association (1999). Quotes about music therapy. Last accessed on 5/30/08 at: http://www.musictherapy.org/quotes.html.

American Psychiatric Association (2000). *Diagnostic and Statistical Manual of Mental Disorders IV, Text Revision.* American Psychiatric Association: Washington, DC.

Avalon Hills (2008). Avalon Hills Inpatient Treatment Center. Last accessed on 5/30/08 at: http://www.avalonhills.org/programs/

Awake (1999). Facial Mark: Nigeria's fading 'identity card'. Last accessed on 5/30/08 at http://www.watchtower.org/e/19990108/article_01.htm

Balch, W., Bowman, K., & Mohler, L. (1992). Music-dependent memory in immediate and delayed word recall. *Memory and Cognition*, 20, 21-28.

Balch, W., & Lewis, B. (1996). Music-dependent memory: the roles of tempo change and mood mediation. *Journal of Experimental Psychology: Learning, Memory, and Cognition*, 22, 1354-1363.

Bauserman, S. (1998). Treatment of persons who self-mutilate with dialectical behavior therapy. Psychiatric Rehabilitation Skills, 2(2), 149-157.

Beers Miller, R. (2007). The role of response art in the case of an adolescent survivor of developmental trauma. *Art Therapy: Journal of the American Art Association*, 24(4), 184-190.

Briks, A. (2007). Art therapy with adolescents: vehicle to engagement and transformation. *The Canadian Art Therapy Association Journal*, 20(1), 2-15.

Brown, L.K., Houck, C.D., Hadley, W.S., & Lescano, C.M. (2005). Self-cutting and sexual risk among adolescents in intensive psychiatric treatment. *Psychiatric Services*, 56(2), 216-218.

Campbell, K. (2007). Review of my recovery zone: an expressive journal for myself. *Art Therapy: Journal of the American Art Therapy Association*, 24(3), 144-145.

Cohen, B., Barnes, M., & Rankin, A. (1995). *Managing traumatic stress through art: Drawing from the center.* Lutherville, MD: Sidran Press.

Cohn, M., Mehl, M., & Pennebaker, J. (2004). Linguistic markers of psychological change surrounding September 11, 2001. *Psychological Science*, 15(10), 687-693.

Degelman, D., & Price, N. (2002). Tattoos and ratings of personal characteristics. *Psychological Reports*, 90(2), 507-514.

Diamond-Raab, L., & Orrell-Valente, J. (2002). Art therapy, psychodrama, and verbal therapy: an integrative model of group therapy in the treatment of adolescents with anorexia nervosa and bulimia nervosa. *Child and Adolescent Psychiatric Clinics*, 11, 343-364.

Dick, B. (1999). What early AA was really like. Last accessed on 5/30/08 at: http://www.dickb.com/index.shtml

Family Therapy (2006). Therapist Profile: Michael White. Retrieved on 10/3/07 at: http://www.abacon.com/famtherapy/white.html.

Favazza, A. (1998). The coming of age of self-mutilation. *Journal of Nervous and Mental Disease*, 186(5), 259-268.

Favazza, A.R. (1987) *Bodies under siege: Self-mutilation in culture and psychiatry*. Baltimore, MD: John Hopkins University Press.

Favazza, A., DeRosear, L., & Conterio, K. (1989). Self-mutilation and eating disorders. *Suicide and Life Threatening Behaviors*, 19, 352-361.

Fenning, S., Carlson, G., & Fenning, S. (1995). Contagious self-mutilation. *Journal of the American Academy of Child and Adolescent Psychiatry*, 37, 211-217.

Foa, E., Molnar, C., & Cashman, L. (1995). Change in rape narratives during exposure therapy for posttraumtic stress disorder. *Journal of Traumatic Stress*, 8(4), 675-681.

Folkman, S., Lazarus, R., Gruen, R., & DeLongis, A. (1986). Appraisal, coping, health status, and psychological symptoms. *Journal of Personality and Social Psychology*, 50(3), 571-579.

Green, C., Knysz, W., & Tsuang, M. (2000). A homeless person with bipolar disorder and a history of self-mutilation. *American Journal of Psychiatry*, 157(9), 1392-1397.

Gregory, K., & Vessey, J. (2004). Bibliotherapy: A strategy to help students with bullying. *The Journal of School Nursing*, 20 (3), 127-133.

Goldenberg, & Goldenberg (2008). *Family Therapy: An Overview* (5th edition). New York: Brooks-Cole/Wadsworth.

Gould, M. (2004). Suicide Contagion. The Suicide
and Mental Health Association International
(SMHAI). Last accessed on 5/30/08 at: http://
suicideandmentalhealthassociationinternational.org/
suiconclust.html

Grief, J., Hewitt, W., &Armstrong, M. (1999). Tattooing
and Body Piercing: body art practices among college
students. *Clinical Nursing Research*, 8(4), 368-385.

Hanieh, E., & Walker, B. (2007). Photography as a measure
of constricted construing: the experience of depression
through a camera. *Journal of Constructivist Psychology*, 20,
183-200.

Havsteen-Franklin, D. (2007). Differentiating the ego-
personality and internal other in art psychotherapy
with patients with borderline personality disorder.
Psychodynamic Practice, 13(1), 59-83.

Herpertz, S., Sass, H., & Favazza, A. (1997). Impulsivity in
self-mutilative behavior: psychometric and biological
findings. *Journal of Psychiatry Research*, 31(4) 451-
465.

Huband, N. & Tantam, D. (2004). Repeated Self-Wounding:
Women's recollection of pathways to cutting and of
the value of different interventions. *Psychology and
Psychotherapy: Theory, Research, and Practice*, 77, 413-
428.

Krysinksa, K., Heller, T.S., & De Leo, D. (2006). Suicide and
deliberate self-harm in personality disorders. Current
Opinions in Psychiatry, 19(1), 95-101.

Levenkron, S. (1998). *Cutting: Understanding and Overcoming Self-Mutilation.* New York: Norton and Co., Inc.

Levy, K.N. (2005). The implications of attachment theory and research for understanding borderline personality disorder. *Development and Psychopathology,* 17, 959-986.

Martino, S. (2008 in press). Perceptions of people with visible piercings. *Psychological Reports.*

Mayo Clinic staff (2006). Signs and Symptoms: What cutting is and isn't. Last accessed on 5/30/08 at: http://www.mayoclinic.com/health/self-injury/DS00775/DSECTION=2.

Lee, R., Epplar, C., Kendal, N., & Latty, C. (2001). Critical incidents in the professional lives of first year MFT students. *Contemporary Family Therapy,* 23(1), 51-61.

Linehan (1997) Dialectical behavior therapy for borderline personality disorder. From *The Journal,* 8(1). Retrieved on 5/30/08 at http://www.dbtselfhelp.com/html/linehandbt.html

Linehan, M. (1993). *Cognitive-Behavioral Treatment of Borderline Personality Disorder.* New York: Guilford Press.

Luiselli, J., Evans, T., & Boyce, D. (1986). Pharmacological assessment and comprehensive behavioral intervention in a case of pediatric self-injury. *Journal of Clinical Child Psychology,* 15 (4), 323-326.

Lyshak, R., Singer, P., St. John, P, & Chemtob, C. (2007). Art therapy for adolescents with posttraumatic stress disorder symptoms: A pilot study. *Journal of the American Art Therapy Association*, 24(4), 163-169.

Madigan, S. (2007). Chitter-Chatter: The Language of our Lives Therapeutic Conversations with Internalized Problem Dialogues. Last accessed on 5/30/08 at: http://www.yaletownfamilytherapy.com

McGlynn, A., & Locke, B. (1997). A 25-year follow-up of a punishment program for severe self-injury. *Behavioral Interventions*, 12 (4), 203-207.

Nevid, J., Rathus, S., & Greene, B. (2005). *Abnormal Psychology in a Changing World* (6th Edition). New York: Prentice Hall.

Nolen-Hoeksema, S., & Corte, C. (2004). Gender and self-regulation. In *Handbook of self-regulation: Research, theory, and applications*. Baumeister, Roy F.; Vohs, Kathleen D.(Eds). Guilford Press: New York, NY, 411-421.

Parry, A. & Doan, R. (1994). *Story Revisions: Narrative Therapy in the Postmodern World*. New York: Guilford Press.

Petersen, S., Bull, C., Propst, O., Dettinger, S., & Detweiler, L. (2005). Narrative therapy to prevent illness-related stress disorder. *Journal of Counseling and Development*, 83, 41-47.

Pifalo, T. (2002). Pulling out the thorns: art therapy with sexually abused children and adolescents. *Art Therapy: Journal of the American Art Therapy Association, 19*(1)12-22.

Ross, S., & Heath, N.L. (2003). Two models of adolescent self-mutilation. *Suicide and Life-Threatening Behavior, 33*(3), 277-287.

Schinagle, M. (2002). Recurrent suicide attempts, self-mutilation, and binge/purge behavior: A case report. *Harvard Review Psychiatry, 10,* 353-363.

Self Harm (2006). *Mental Health Foundation.* Retrieved 10/3/07 at: http://www.mentalhealth.org.uk/information/mental-health-a-z/self-harm/

Segal-Trivitz, Y., Bloch, Y., Goldburt, Y., Sobol-Havia, D., Levkovitch, Y., & Ratzoni, G. (2006). Comparison of symptoms and treatments of adults and adolescents with borderline personality disorder. *International Journal of Adolescent Medicine and Health, 18*(2), 215-220.

Shapiro, S. (1991). Affect integration in psychoanalysis: A clinical approach to self-destructive behavior. *Bulletin of the Menninger Clinic, 55,* 363-374.

Shaw, S. (2006). Certainty, revision, and ambivalence: a qualitative investigation into women's journeys to stop self-injuring. *Women & Therapy, 29*(1), 153-177.

Silk, K. (2008). Augmenting psychotherapy for borderline personality disorder: the STEPPS program. American *Journal of Psychiatry, 165*(4), 413-415.

Smith, S., Anderson-Hanley, C., Langrock, A., & Compas, B. (2005). The effects of journaling for women with newly diagnosed breast cancer. Psycho-Oncology, 14, 1075-1082.

Smith, G., Cox, D., & Saradijan, J. (1999). *Women and Self Harm: Understanding, Coping, and Healing from Self-Injury*. New York: Routledge.

Soloff, P., Lis, J., Kelly, T., Cornelius, J., & Ulrich, R. (1994). Self-mutilation and suicidal behavior in borderline personality disorder. *Journal of Personality Disorders*, 8(4), 257-267.

Sommers-Flanagan, J. (2007). The development and evolution of person-centered expressive art therapy: a conversation with Natalie Rogers. *Journal of Counseling and Development*, 85, 120-125.

Stone, M. (1998). Journaling with clients. *The Journal of Individual Psychology*, 54(4), 535-545.

Strauch, M. (2007). Promoting insight and change through the systematic use of early recollections with role-play, art, and cognitive reconstruction. *The Journal of Individual Psychology*, 63(2), 205-213.

Swadi, H. (2004). Self-mutilation among adolescents and youth: some clinical perspectives. *New Zealand Family Physician*, 31(6), 374-377.

Sweig, T. (2000). Women healing women: time-limited, psychoeducational group therapy for childhood sexual abuse survivors. *Art Therapy: Journal of the American Art Therapy Association*, 17 (4), 255-264.

Turner, V.J. (2002). *Secret Scars: Uncovering and Understanding the Addiction.* Center City, MN: Hazelden.

Wagner, M. (2001). Behavioral characteristics related to substance abuse and risk-taking, sensation- seeking, anxiety sensitivity and self-reinforcement. *Addictive Behaviors*, 26, 115-120.

Wagoner, D., & Wijekumar, K. (2004). Improving self-awareness of nutrition and lifestyle practices through on-line journaling. *Journal of Nutrition Education and Behavior*, 36, 211-212.

Waska, R.T. (1998). Self-mutilation, substance abuse, and the psychoanalytic approach: Four cases. *American Journal of Psychotherapy*, 52(1), 18-27.

Weiser, J. (2001). The Techniques of Phototherapy. Last accessed on 5/30/08 at: http://www.phototherapy-centre.com/five_techniques.htm#fivetech

Weiser, J. (2007). Using PhotoTherapy techniques in Art Therapy and other counseling practices. *Canadian Art Therapy Association Newsletter*, 6(4), 4-7.

Weiser, J. (2008). Photo Therapy: Unlock your psyche with personal snapshots and family photographs. *Taliese: Jumeirah Group Wellness Magazine*, 2, 59-62.

White, M. An Outline of Narrative Therapy. Last accessed 5/30/08 at: http://www.massey.ac.nz/~alock/virtual/white.htm

Zila, L., & Kiselica, M.S. (2001). Understanding and counseling self-mutilation in female adolescents and young adults. *Journal of Counseling and Development, 79,* 46-52.

About the Author

Sara Martino, Ph.D., is Assistant Professor of Psychology in the School of Social and Behavioral Sciences at the Richard Stockton College. She teaches an array of courses including Abnormal Psychology, Experimental Psychology, and Gender and Aggressive Behavior. Martino lives with her family in Medford, New Jersey.

The future of publishing...today!

Apprentice House is the country's only campus-based, student-staffed book publishing company. Directed by professors and industry professionals, it is a nonprofit activity of the Communication Department at Loyola University Maryland.

Using state-of-the-art technology and an experiential learning model of education, Apprentice House publishes books in untraditional ways. This dual responsibility as publishers and educators creates an unprecedented collaborative environment among faculty and students, while teaching tomorrow's editors, designers, and marketers. Outside of class, progress on book projects is carried forth by the AH Book Publishing Club, a co-curricular campus organization supported by Loyola University's Office of Student Activities.

Student Project Team for *Scars*:
    Jessica Guiton, '08
    Jessica Hofmann, '09
    Julia Sherrier, '08

Eclectic and provocative, Apprentice House titles intend to entertain as well as spark dialogue on a variety of topics. Contributions are welcomed to sustain the press's work and are tax deductible to the fullest extent allowed by the IRS.

To learn more about Apprentice House books or to obtain submission guidelines, please visit www.ApprenticeHouse.com.

Apprentice House
c/o Communication Department
Loyola University Maryland
4501 N. Charles Street
Baltimore, MD 21210
Ph: 410-617-5265 • Fax: 410-617-5040
info@apprenticehouse.com

CPSIA information can be obtained
at www.ICGtesting.com
Printed in the USA
BVHW030220050719
552672BV00001B/33/P